Easy Party Cakes

Easy Party Cakes

30 original and fun designs for every occasion

DEBBIE BROWN

NEW HOLLAND

For my very special parents, Pam & Ray Herbert, with love.

Reprinted in 2010
First published in 2007 by New Holland Publishers (UK) Ltd
London · Cape Town · Sydney · Auckland

Garfield House, 86–88 Edgware Road, London, W2 2EA, United Kingdom
www.newhollandpublishers.com

80 McKenzie Street, Cape Town 8001, South Africa

Unit 1, 66 Gibbes Street, Chatswood, NSW, Australia, 2067

218 Lake Road, Northcote, Auckland, New Zealand

5 7 9 10 8 6 4

ISBN 978 1 84537 618 5

Editor: Ruth Hamilton
Design: AG&G Books
y: Edward Allwright (p6–15) and Shona Wood
Production: Marion Storz
itorial Direction: Rosemary Wilkinson

Reproduction by Pica Digital PTE Ltd, Singapore
Printed and bound by Times Offset, Malaysia

ACKNOWLEDGEMENTS

My appreciation and thanks to Renshaw's for supplying all the
good quality Regalice sugarpaste used throughout this book.
To Ruth Hamilton for her patience, careful editing and professionalism.
To Shona Wood for her good humour and great pictures during our shoots.
To my husband Paul, for his love and support always.

Contents

Introduction

Flicking through most craft books, especially when you really haven't a clue about how something is made, can really be quite off-putting. I completely understand that there are many who do actually put the books down thinking they cannot possibly do any of the projects. However, I promise that with these clear instructions, good quality ingredients and a little time and patience, you will produce something to be proud of.

This book contains some simple designs that a beginner would be confident enough to tackle and some that are more involved, but I find through teaching over many years that a complete beginner sometimes has a natural ability and produces something that is superior to someone who has been 'sugarcrafting' for many years.

For experienced cake decorators, there are nice ideas both simple and more advanced to inspire and experiment with new techniques. This collection of cake designs are a perfect mix for adults and children, each full of fun and humour to make a talking point at any special celebration and ensuring the day remains memorable.

Bear in mind that it is a great compliment to be given a cake that someone has taken valuable time and effort to produce just for them, plus it stops the headache of finding that unique present by making one instead!

Just remember to have fun.

Basic Recipes

I would always recommend making your own cake base, as shop-bought versions do not produce the same results. Many specialist cake decorating suppliers will supply ready-made sugarpaste, modelling paste, royal icing and other ingredients, but you will find recipes for making your own in this section. All spoon measures are level unless otherwise stated.

MADEIRA SPONGE CAKE

I prefer to use a Madeira sponge cake recipe for all my cakes as you need a cake which is moist and light, but still suitable for carving and sculpting without crumbling. Shop-bought cake mixes and ready-made cakes will not produce the same results, as they are often too soft and crumbly to withstand sculpting into different shapes. For each of the cakes in this book, refer to the cake chart on page 10–11 for specific quantities and baking times, then follow the method given below.

1 Preheat the oven to 150–160°C / 325°F / Gas mark 3, then grease and line your baking tin.
2 Sift the self-raising and plain (all-purpose) flours together in a bowl.
3 Soften the butter and place in a food mixer or large mixing bowl with the caster (superfine) sugar and beat until the mixture is pale and fluffy.
4 Add the eggs to the mixture one at a time with a spoonful of the flour, beating well after each addition. Add a few drops of vanilla extract.
5 Using a spatula or large spoon, fold the remaining flour into the mixture.
6 Spoon the mixture into the tin, then make a dip in the top of the mixture using the back of a spoon.
7 Bake in the centre of the oven for the time stated in the cake chart (see page 10–11), or until a skewer inserted in the centre comes out clean.
8 Leave to cool in the tin for five minutes, then turn out onto a wire rack and leave to cool completely. When cold, store in an airtight container or double wrap in clingfilm (plastic wrap) for at least eight hours, allowing the texture to settle before use.

MADEIRA CAKE VARIATIONS

CHOCOLATE MARBLE CAKE

Before spooning the cake mixture into the tin, fold in 200g (7oz) of melted chocolate until marbled. Fold in completely for a light chocolate cake.

CHOCOLATE ORANGE MARBLE CAKE

Follow the instructions for a Chocolate Marble Cake, adding the grated rind and juice of one organic orange.

LEMON CAKE

Add the grated rind and juice of one organic lemon to the cake mixture.

ORANGE AND LEMON CAKE

Add the grated rind of one organic orange and one lemon to the cake mixture and add a squeeze of orange juice.

Madeira sponge cake

COFFEE CAKE

Add two tablespoons of coffee essence to the cake mixture.

ALMOND

Add 1 teaspoon of almond essence and 2–3 tablespoons of ground almonds to the cake mixture.

BUTTERCREAM

Buttercream is very versatile as it is suitable as a cake filling as well as for creating a crumb coat. This seals the cake to stop it from drying out, and provides a good adhesive base for the sugarpaste coating. For intricately sculpted cakes, leave the buttercream crumb coat to set firmly, then add a little more or rework the surface to soften so that the sugarpaste will stick to the cake.

Makes 625g / 1¼lb / 3¾c

- 175g / 6oz / ¾c unsalted butter, softened
- 2–3 Tbsp milk
- 1 tsp vanilla extract
- 450g / 1lb / 3¼c icing (powdered) sugar, sifted

1 Place the softened butter, milk and vanilla extract into a mixer. Add the icing sugar a little at a time, mixing on medium speed, until light, fluffy and pale in colour.
2 Store in an airtight container and use within 10 days. Bring to room temperature and beat again before use.

BUTTERCREAM VARIATIONS

CHOCOLATE
Add 90g (3oz) of good-quality melted chocolate, or use 3–4 tablespoons of cocoa powder mixed to a paste with milk.

ORANGE OR LEMON CURD
Add 2–3 tablespoons of orange or lemon curd.

COFFEE
Add 2–3 tablespoons of coffee essence.

RASPBERRY
Add 3–4 tablespoons of seedless raspberry jam.

ALMOND
Add 1 teaspoon almond essence.

Sugarpaste blocks

SUGARPASTE

Good-quality ready-made sugarpaste is easy to use, produces good results and comes in a range of colours. It is readily available in large supermarkets and through specialist cake decorating outlets. However, if you prefer to make your own sugarpaste, try the following recipe. CMC is an abbreviation of Carboxymethyl Cellulose, an edible thickener widely used in the food industry. Check that it is food grade C1000P/E466. Gum tragacanth can be used as an alternative.

Makes 625g / 1¼lb / 3¾c

- 1 egg white made up from dried egg albumen
- 2 Tbsp liquid glucose
- 625g / 1¼lb / 3¾c icing (powdered) sugar
- A little white vegetable fat, if required
- A pinch of CMC or gum tragacanth, if required

1 Put the egg white and liquid glucose into a bowl, using a warm spoon for the liquid glucose.
2 Sift the icing sugar into the bowl, adding a little at a time and stirring until the mixture thickens.

3 Turn out onto a work surface dusted liberally with icing sugar and knead the paste until soft, smooth and pliable. If the paste is a little dry and cracked, fold in some vegetable fat and knead again. If the paste is soft and sticky, add a little more icing sugar or a pinch of CMC or gum tragacanth to stabilize.
4 Put immediately into a polythene bag and store in an airtight container. Keep at room temperature or refrigerate and use within a week. Bring back to room temperature and knead thoroughly before use. Home-made sugarpaste can be frozen for up to 3 months.

ROYAL ICING

Royal icing is used to pipe details such as hair, fur effect, etc. It is also used to stick items together, as when it dries it holds items firmly in place. Ready-made royal icing or powder form (follow instructions on the packet) can be obtained from supermarkets. To make your own, use this recipe.

Makes 75g (2½oz)

- 1 tsp egg albumen
- 1 Tbsp water
- 65–70g / 2¼oz / ½c icing (powdered) sugar

1 Put the egg albumen into a bowl. Add the water and stir until dissolved. Beat in the icing sugar a little at a time until the icing is firm, glossy and forms peaks if a spoon is pulled out.
2 To stop the icing from forming a crust, place a damp cloth over the top of the bowl until you are ready to use it, or transfer to an airtight container and refrigerate.

EDIBLE GLUE

This recipe makes a strong edible glue which works extremely well. Alternatively, ready-made edible glue can be purchased from specialist cake decorating outlets.

- ¼ tsp CMC powder or gum tragacanth
- 2 Tbsp water

1 Mix the CMC with water and leave to stand until the powder is fully absorbed. The glue should be smooth and have a soft dropping consistency.
2 If the glue thickens after a few days, add a few drops more water. Store in an airtight container in the refrigerator and use within one week.
3 To use, brush a thin coat over the surface of the item you wish to glue, leave for a few moments to become tacky, and then press in place.

MODELLING PASTE

Modelling paste is used for creating figures and other smaller modelled items as it is more flexible. This quick and easy recipe makes a high quality modelling paste, which has been used throughout the book.

- 450g (1lb) sugarpaste (see page 8)
- 1 tsp CMC powder or gum tragacanth

1 Knead the CMC into sugarpaste. The sugarpaste starts to thicken as soon as CMC is incorporated so it can be used immediately. More thickening will occur gradually over a period of 24 hours.
2 The amount of CMC can be varied depending on usage; a firmer paste is more suitable for limbs, miniature modelling etc., so a little more can

be added. This tends to dry the paste much faster, so modelling should be done quickly. Simpler or larger modelled pieces should need less CMC. It is also dependent on room temperature, atmospheric conditions, etc., so adjust accordingly. Store in an airtight container and use within two weeks for best results.

QUICK PASTILLAGE

Pastillage is a fast-drying paste that dries much harder than other pastes so is suitable for items that need extra strength, i.e., the Musical Notes frame that joins the two cakes (see pages 79–81) and also the upright poles used in the Prize Allotment design (see pages 122–125).

Makes 260g (9oz) pastillage

- 2 tsp CMC powder or gum tragacanth
- 260g (9oz) royal icing

1 Mix the CMC or gum tragacanth into stiff-peaked royal icing. The mixture will thicken immediately. Knead on a work surface sprinkled liberally with icing sugar until the mixture forms a paste and is smooth and crack-free.
2 Keep in an airtight container and store in the refrigerator. Bring back to room temperature before use.

EDIBLE GLITTER

There is a lot of choice available through specialist cake decorating outlets for edible sparkling powders, but the glitters tend to be non-toxic food-safe, which I recommend be removed before serving. If you prefer to use something edible, try this quick and simple glitter recipe.

1 Mix equal parts (¼–½ tsp) gum arabic, water and your chosen edible metallic or sparkle powder food colouring. The mixture should look like thick paint.
2 Place a non-stick ovenproof liner/sheet onto a baking tray and brush the mixture over the surface. The mixture may congeal, so brush it out as thinly as possible. Bake on a very low heat for around ten minutes, until dry and starting to peel away from the liner.
3 Remove from oven and leave to cool. Lift with a palette knife and place into a sieve. Gently push through the sieve to produce small glitter particles. Store in a food-safe container.

SUGAR STICKS

These are used as edible supports, mainly to help hold modelled heads in place, but they can also be used for a variety of other purposes – flagpoles, for example – depending on their size.

Makes around 10–20 sugar sticks

- 1 level tsp stiff peak royal icing
- ¼ tsp CMC or gum tragacanth

1 Knead the CMC or gum tragacanth into the royal icing until the mixture forms a paste. Either roll it out and cut it into different sized strips of various lengths using a plain-bladed knife, or roll individual thin paste sausages. Let dry on a sheet of foam, preferably overnight. When dry, store in an airtight container.

Cake Chart

To create the delicious cakes in this book you will need to refer to this cake chart for specific quantities and baking times, then simply follow the appropriate method given on page 7.

CONSTRUCTION SITE

20cm (8in) square tin

- Unsalted butter, softened 340g/12oz/1½c
- Caster (superfine) sugar 340g/12oz/1¾c
- Large eggs 6
- Self-raising flour 340g/12oz/3c
- Plain (all-purpose) flour 145g/5oz/1⅓c

Baking time 1¼–1½ hours

SLEEPY TED

2L (4 pint), 1L (2 pint) and 15cm (6in) square tin

Put half of mix into large bowl and then divide the remainder between the small bowl and the square tin

- Unsalted butter, softened 450g/1lb/2c
- Caster (superfine) sugar 450g/1lb/2⅓c
- Large eggs 8
- Self-raising flour 450g/1lb/4c
- Plain (all-purpose) flour 175g/6oz/1½c

Baking time Square tin and small bowl 1–1¼ hours, large bowl 1¼–1½ hours

CIRCUS TRAIN
WATER RIDE

25 x 15cm (10 x 6in) oblong tin

- Unsalted butter, softened 225g/8oz/1c
- Caster (superfine) sugar 225g/8oz/1c + 2 Tbsp
- Large eggs 4
- Self-raising flour 225g/8oz/2c
- Plain (all-purpose) flour 115g/4oz/1c

Baking time 1–1¼ hours

PONY PALACE

20cm (8in) and 10cm (4in) round tins

- Unsalted butter, softened 340g/12oz/1½c
- Caster (superfine) sugar 340g/12oz/1¾c
- Large eggs 6
- Self-raising flour 340g/12oz/3c
- Plain (all-purpose) flour 145g/5oz/1⅓c

Baking time Large tin 1¼–1½ hours, small tin 1–1¼ hours

PLAYFUL PUPPIES

12 hole bun tin

- Unsalted butter, softened 115g/4oz/½c
- Caster (superfine) sugar 115g/4oz/⅔c
- Large eggs 2
- Self-raising flour 115g/4oz/1c
- Plain (all-purpose) flour 60g/2oz/½c

Baking time 30 mins

NO MORE 9 TO 5

2 x 15cm (6in) round tins

- Unsalted butter, softened 285g/10oz/1⅓c
- Caster (superfine) sugar 285g/10oz/1½c
- Large eggs 5
- Self-raising flour 285g/10oz/2½c
- Plain (all-purpose) flour 115g/4oz/1c

Baking time 1–1¼ hours

CHAMPAGNE BUBBLES

1 x 10cm (4in) round tin and 2 x 15cm (6in) round tins

- Unsalted butter, softened 340g/12oz/1½c
- Caster (superfine) sugar 340g/12oz/1¾c
- Large eggs 6
- Self-raising flour 340g/12oz/3c
- Plain (all-purpose) flour 145g/5oz/1⅓c

Baking time 2 x 15cm (6in) round tins 1¼–1½ hours, 1 x 10cm (4in) round tin 1–1¼ hours

LUCKY NUMBERS
DANCING PRESENTS
BAKING DAY

20cm (8in) square tin

- Unsalted butter, softened 285g/10oz/1⅓c
- Caster (superfine) sugar 285g/10oz/1½c
- Large eggs 5
- Self-raising flour 285g/10oz/2½c
- Plain (all-purpose) flour 115g/4oz/1c

Baking time 1¼–1½ hours

WASH DAY

25cm (10in) square tin

- Unsalted butter, softened 285g/10oz/1⅓c
- Caster (superfine) sugar 285g/10oz/1½c
- Large eggs 5
- Self-raising flour 285g/10oz/2½c
- Plain (all-purpose) flour 115g/4oz/1c

Baking time 1–1¼ hours

WHITE VAN MAN

25cm (10in) square tin

- Unsalted butter, softened 340g/12oz/1½c
- Caster (superfine) sugar 340g/12oz/1¾c
- Large eggs 6
- Self-raising flour 340g/12oz/3c
- Plain (all-purpose) flour 145g/5oz/1⅓c

Baking time 1¼–1½ hours

PARTY HATS

3 x 15cm (6in), 2 x 12cm (5in) and 1 x 10cm (4in) round tins

- Unsalted butter, softened 450g/1lb/2c
- Caster (superfine) sugar 450g/1lb/2⅓c
- Large eggs 8
- Self-raising flour 450g/1lb/4c
- Plain (all-purpose) flour 175g/6oz/1½c

Baking time 1–1¼ hours

PRIZE ALLOTMENT
BEACH HUT
30cm (12in) square tin
- Unsalted butter, softened 340g/12oz/1½c
- Caster (superfine) sugar 340g/12oz/1¾c
- Large eggs 6
- Self-raising flour 340g/12oz/3c
- Plain (all-purpose) flour 145g/5oz/1⅓c

Baking time 1–1¼ hours

TECHNO FREAK
1 x 15cm (6in) and 1 x 20cm (8in) square tins
Put ¼ of mixture in small tin, then remainder into larger tin
- Unsalted butter, softened 450g/1lb/2c
- Caster (superfine) sugar 450g/1lb/2⅓c
- Large eggs 8
- Self-raising flour 450g/1lb/4c
- Plain (all-purpose) flour 175g/6oz/1½c

Baking time 20cm (8in) square tin 1½ hours, 15cm (6in) sqaure tin 1–1¼ hours

SUN, SEA AND SNORKELLING
20cm (8in) round tin
- Unsalted butter, softened 225g/8oz/1c
- Caster (superfine) sugar 225g/8oz/1c + 2 Tbsp
- Large eggs 4
- Self-raising flour 225g/8oz/2c
- Plain (all-purpose) flour 115g/4oz/1c

Baking time 1–1¼ hours

TRAVEL BUG
25cm (10in) round tin
- Unsalted butter, softened 340g/12oz/1½c
- Caster (superfine) sugar 340g/12oz/1¾c
- Large eggs 6
- Self-raising flour 340g/12oz/3c
- Plain (all-purpose) flour 145g/5oz/1⅓c

Baking time 1–1¼ hours

QUEENIE MUM
15cm (6in) round tin and 20cm (8in) square tin
- Unsalted butter, softened 400g/14oz/1¾c
- Caster (superfine) sugar 400g/14oz/2c
- Large eggs 7
- Self-raising flour 400g/14oz/3½c
- Plain (all-purpose) flour 175g/6oz/1½c

Baking time 1¼–1½ hours

THE 19TH HOLE
20cm (8in) and 12cm (5in) round tins
- Unsalted butter, softened 340g/12oz/1½c
- Caster (superfine) sugar 340g/12oz/1¾c
- Large eggs 6
- Self-raising flour 340g/12oz/3c
- Plain (all-purpose) flour 145g/5oz/1⅓c

Baking time 20cm (8in) round tin 1¼–1½ hours, 12cm (5in) round tin 1–1¼ hours

POT OF GOLD
2L (4pint) ovenproof bowl and 20cm (8in) round tin
- Unsalted butter, softened 400g/14oz/1¾c
- Caster (superfine) sugar 400g/14oz/2c
- Large eggs 7
- Self-raising flour 400g/14oz/3½c
- Plain (all-purpose) flour 175g/6oz/1½c

Baking time 1¼–1½ hours

JUNK FOOD MOUNTAIN
2 x 20cm (8in) round tins
- Unsalted butter, softened 450g/1lb/2c
- Caster (superfine) sugar 450g/1lb/2⅓c
- Large eggs 8
- Self-raising flour 450g/1lb/4c
- Plain (all-purpose) flour 175g/6oz/1½c

Baking time 1¼–1½ hours

CASTLE RUIN
20cm (8in) round tin
- Unsalted butter, softened 225g/8oz/1c
- Caster (superfine) sugar 225g/8oz/1c + 2 Tbsp
- Large eggs 4
- Self-raising flour 225g/8oz/2c
- Plain (all-purpose) flour 115g/4oz/1c

Baking time 1¼–1½ hours

SUMO SUITS
2 x 1L (2 pint) ovenproof bowls
- Unsalted butter, softened 340g/12oz/1½c
- Caster (superfine) sugar 340g/12oz/1¾c
- Large eggs 6
- Self-raising flour 340g/12oz/3c
- Plain (all-purpose) flour 145g/5oz/1⅓c

Baking time 1½–1¾ hours

PAMPERED PET
25cm (10in) round tin
- Unsalted butter, softened 340g/12oz/1½c
- Caster (superfine) sugar 340g/12oz/1¾c
- Large eggs 6
- Self-raising flour 340g/12oz/3c
- Plain (all-purpose) flour 145g/5oz/1⅓c

Baking time 1¼–1½ hours

BEER ON TAP
3 x 15cm (6in) round tins
- Unsalted butter, softened 340g/12oz/1½c
- Caster (superfine) sugar 340g/12oz/1¾c
- Large eggs 6
- Self-raising flour 340g/12oz/3c
- Plain (all-purpose) flour 145g/5oz/1⅓c

Baking time 1–1¼ hours

FISHING TROPHY
23cm (9in) square tin
- Unsalted butter, softened 340g/12oz/1½c
- Caster (superfine) sugar 340g/12oz/1¾c
- Large eggs 6
- Self-raising flour 340g/12oz/3c
- Plain (all-purpose) flour 145g/5oz/1⅓c

Baking time 1¼–1½ hours

MUSICAL NOTES
4 x 1L (2 pint) ovenproof bowls
- Unsalted butter, softened 450g/1lb/2c
- Caster (superfine) sugar 450g/1lb/2⅓c
- Large eggs 8
- Self-raising flour 450g/1lb/4c
- Plain (all-purpose) flour 175g/6oz/1½c

Baking time 1¼–1½ hours

PRINCESS CUPCAKES
15cm (6in) round tin and 10 cupcake cakes in bun tin
Two thirds fill each cake case then put remainder of mixture into the round tin
- Unsalted butter, softened 285g/10oz/1⅓c
- Caster (superfine) sugar 285g/10oz/1½c
- Large eggs 5
- Self-raising flour 285g/10oz/2½c
- Plain (all-purpose) flour 115g/4oz/1c

Baking time Cupcakes 30 mins, 15cm (6in) round tin 1¼–1½ hours

Basic Techniques

Cake decorating is easier than it looks, although it can seem a little daunting if you are a complete beginner. This section shows you a few simple, basic techniques that will help you achieve great results and professional-looking cakes.

SCULPTING A CAKE

The first rule of cake sculpting is to have a moist but firm sponge cake that will not crumble. I recommend that you follow the recipes and method given in this book for a Madeira sponge cake (see page 7). If you are tempted to buy a cake mix or a ready-baked cake, make sure that it won't crumble away as soon as you start to cut into it. Ready-made cakes are really only suitable for projects involving minimal sculpting and stacking of layers.

Use a serrated knife for cake carving. When trimming away the crust of a cake, keep the cake as level as possible so there are no problems with balance if the cake is being stacked. Use a ruler for straight cuts and be aware of the knife blade, keeping it in the correct position for the cut you need.

ROLLING OUT SUGARPASTE

Sugarpaste can be rolled out successfully on any even food-safe work surface, but I recommend that you use a large polypropylene board and rolling pin, both of which have tough, smooth surfaces.

Start by dusting your worksurface lightly with icing (powdered) sugar. Knead the sugarpaste thoroughly, until soft and warm. Sugarpaste can start to dry out when exposed to the air, so roll out as quickly and evenly as possible to a covering thickness of around 3–4mm (⅛in), moving the paste around after each roll using a sprinkling of icing (powdered) sugar. Make sure there isn't a build up of sugarpaste or icing (powdered) sugar on either your board or your rolling pin, to help keep the sugarpaste perfectly smooth. Sugarpaste can stick to the work surface very quickly. If this happens, re-knead and start again.

COLOURING SUGARPASTE

Some brands of ready-made sugarpaste are available in a range of colours but I usually prefer to mix my own colours. The best food colourings are obtainable as a paste or concentrated liquid. Avoid the watery liquid food colourings and powder colours, unless you want to achieve very pale shades. Powder food colours are usually only used to brush over the surface of dried sugarpaste to enhance certain areas.

The best way to apply food colour paste is with the tip of a knife. Simply dab a block of sugarpaste with the end of a knife (if you are creating a new colour, remember to keep a record of how many "dabs" of paste you use). Add a little at a time until the required shade is achieved. Knead thoroughly after each addition until the colour is even. Bear in mind that the colour will deepen slightly on standing, so be careful not to add too much.

If you wish to colour a large amount of sugarpaste, colour a small ball first, and then knead into the remaining amount to disperse the colour quickly. Wearing plastic gloves or rubbing a little white vegetable fat over your hands can help when colouring with deep shades, as this can prevent a lot of mess. Some food colours can temporarily stain your hands.

Sculpting a cake

Rolling out sugarpaste

Colouring sugarpaste

COVERING A CAKE BOARD WITH SUGARPASTE

Knead the sugarpaste thoroughly until soft and warm. Roll out to roughly the size and shape of the cake board, using a sprinkling of icing (powdered) sugar and move around after each roll to prevent sticking.

Place the rolling pin on the centre of the rolled out sugarpaste and lift the back half over the top. Hold both ends of the rolling pin, lift and position the sugarpaste against the cake board and unroll over the top. Roll the rolling pin gently over the surface to stick the sugarpaste firmly to the board. If the sugarpaste is still loose, moisten along the outside edge only, using a little water or edible glue on a brush.

Rub the surface with a cake smoother for a smooth, dimple-free surface. Lift the cake board and trim away the excess around the outside

Covering a cake board with sugarpaste

edge using a plain-bladed knife. Keep the knife straight to gain a neat edge, carefully removing any residue along the blade for a clean cut.

COVERING A CAKE WITH SUGARPASTE

Before applying sugarpaste to the buttercream-covered surface of a cake, make sure the buttercream is soft and sticky by reworking a little using a knife, or by adding a little more. Roll the sugarpaste out approximately 15cm (6in) larger than the top of the cake to allow enough icing to cover the sides of the cake. You can lift and position the sugarpaste on the cake as you would to cover a cake board, and then press the sugarpaste gently but firmly in position, smoothing over the surface using your hands. Rub gently with your hands over any small cracks to blend them in. If you have any gaps, stroke the sugarpaste surface to stretch it slightly. Trim away any excess using a plain-bladed knife.

Covering a cake with sugarpaste

OBTAINING A GOOD FINISH

You will invariably find that you have occasional bumps on the surface of your cake or trapped air bubbles. A cake smoother is invaluable for obtaining a perfectly smooth finish for your sugarpaste. Rub firmly but gently

Obtaining a good finish

in a circular motion to remove any small dents or bumps.

Any excess icing (powdered) sugar can be brushed off dried sugarpaste. With stubborn areas, use a slightly damp large soft bristle pastry brush. The moisture will melt the excess, but take care not to wet the surface as streaks may result.

CAKE LAYER CUTTER

It can be quite tricky for a non-professional cake decorator to cut even layers in cakes. Someone with experience usually uses a large serrated knife and just slices through evenly. Some use wooden or plastic strips to the height they need for the layer placed on opposite sides of the cake and use these as cutting guides either using a knife or stretching a food-safe wire or strong thread against them and gently pulling through using a sawing action. For ease, I recommend a cake layer cutter or leveller as they are also called. These are food-safe, height adjustable wires on frames with a raised handle on top that gently slices through your cake. To use, simply place the layer cutter against the cake and gently push backwards and forwards using a sawing action slicing through the cake. Keep the layer cutter level with the work surface to ensure an even cut.

General Equipment

There is a huge selection of cake decorating tools and equipment available now. Listed below are the basic necessities for cake decorating, some of which you likely already have in your kitchen. I've also added some specialist items that can help achieve great results.

1. WORKBOARD You can easily work on any washable, even work surface, but for best results use a non-stick polypropylene work board. They are available in various sizes, with non-slip feet on the reverse.

2. ROLLING PINS Polypropylene rolling pins are available in a variety of lengths, but basic large and small pins are the most useful.

3. SERRATED KNIFE A medium-sized serrated knife is invaluable when sculpting a cake, as it cuts away neatly when using a slight sawing action.

4. PLAIN-BLADED KNIFE Small and medium plain-bladed knives are used to cut through paste cleanly and evenly. Choose knives with ultra-fine blades for neat, clean cuts and make sure the handle and blade are well balanced.

5. PALETTE KNIFE This is used for the smooth spreading of buttercream, and also to help lift modelled pieces easily from a work surface.

6. CAKE SMOOTHER Smoothes the surface of sugarpaste to remove any bumps or indents by rubbing gently in a circular motion.

7. SUGAR SHAKER A handy container filled with icing (powdered) sugar. Used for sprinkling the work surface before rolling out paste.

8. PAINTBRUSHES Available in various sizes, choose good quality sable paintbrushes for painting details. Use a flat-ended brush for dusting powder food colours over the surface of dried paste.

9. LARGE PASTRY BRUSH Invaluable for brushing excess icing (powdered) sugar and crumbs away. When dampened slightly, it will lift any stubborn residue icing (powdered) sugar from the surface quickly and easily.

10. RULER Used for approximate measuring during cake and paste cutting and for indenting neat lines in sugarpaste.

11. SCISSORS Needed for general use of cutting templates, piping bags and some small detailing.

12. PLAIN PIPING TUBES Not only are these tubes used for piping royal icing, they are also used as cutters and indenters. For finer cuts use good quality metal tubes in preference to plastic ones.

13. PAPER PIPING BAGS For use with royal icing. Parchment or greaseproof paper piping bags are available ready-made from cake decorating suppliers.

14. COCKTAIL STICKS Readily available in food-safe wood or plastic form, these are useful for marking any fine detailing in paste.

15. FOAM PIECES Used to support modelled pieces whilst drying, as the air can circulate all around. When the piece is dry, the foam is easily squeezed smaller for easy removal.

16. CUTTERS Available in an array of different styles and shapes. Metal cutters usually have finer, cleaner edges but are more expensive. Some small cutters have plungers to remove the cut out shape.

17. TURNTABLE When working on a cake, placing on a turntable allows you to quickly and easily move the cake around. Some bakers find it invaluable as it lifts the cake to a higher level.

18. FOOD COLOURING Paste colours are suitable for colouring paste and royal icing, while powder colours add a subtle hue when brushed onto the surface of dried sugarpaste.

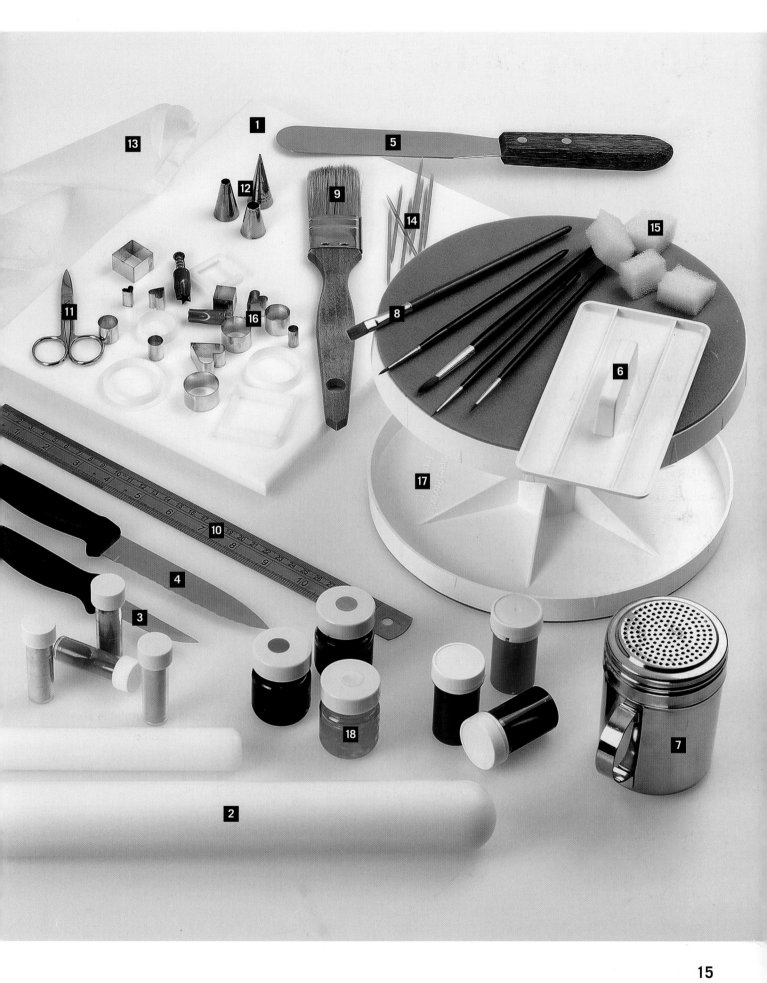

No More 9 to 5

This cake is certain to bring a chuckle of pleasure as retirement looms. Everything that symbolizes the toll of full-time office work relegated to the waste bin!

What you will need

See page 7–11 for all recipes and baking chart

- 2 x 15cm (6in) round cakes
- 30cm (12in) square cake board
- Icing (powdered) sugar in a sugar shaker

Sugarpaste
- 595g (1lb 5oz) pale grey
- 1.9kg (4lb 3¼oz) white

Modelling paste
- 450g (1lb) white
- 240g (8½oz) pale grey
- 315g (11oz) red
- 225g (½lb) blue
- 125g (4½oz) ivory

Royal icing
- 20g (¾oz) black
- 5g (just under ¼oz) white

- 550g (1lb 3½oz / 2¾c) buttercream
- Edible glue and brush

Equipment
- Large rolling pin
- Ruler
- Small plain bladed knife
- Serrated carving knife
- 2.5cm (1in) and 6cm (2½in) circle cutters
- 2 x 12cm (5in) cake cards
- 4 x food safe plastic dowelling
- Pencil
- Cake smoother
- No.1 plain piping tube
- Piping bag
- A few cocktail sticks
- Bone or ball tool
- Foam pieces (for support)

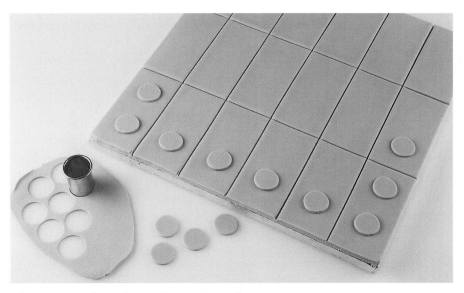

Circles for the tiled effect cake board covering

1 Using a sprinkling of icing sugar to prevent sticking, roll out the grey sugarpaste and cover the cake board completely, trimming excess from around the edge. To mark the oblong-shaped tiles, first indent two lines 10cm (4in) apart down one side of the cake board. Mark across these lines by indenting five lines, 5cm (2in) apart. Roll out the trimmings and cut circles, applying to outside edge tiles only **(see above).**

2 To make the files on which the cake sits, thickly roll out 400g (14oz) of white sugarpaste and cut an oblong measuring 18 x 23cm (7 x 9in). Slice lines to resemble pages around the bottom edge and along each side using a knife. Repeat for the second file. To make the file covers, first roll out 225g (½lb) of red modelling paste and cut a piece to cover around the pages, trimming the edge and leaving the covering around 1cm (½in) larger. Stick this file in position on the cake board using a little edible glue to secure. Repeat for the second file using the blue modelling paste.

3 Trim the crust from each cake and level the tops. Cut a layer in each cake and then stack one on top of the other. Trim the sides of the cake to taper down to the bottom. Sandwich all layers together with buttercream, then spread a layer over the surface to seal the cake and help the sugarpaste stick. Place the cake on one of the cake cards, securing with a little buttercream.

4 Roll out 115g (4oz) of white sugarpaste and cover the top of the cake, trimming neatly around the edge. Because of weight of items placed on top, you will need to dowel the cake and place a cake card on top to stop the layers being compressed, which will result in bulging, spoiling the smooth sugarpaste covering. Push three of the dowels down through the top of the cake and mark each with a pencil level with the top of the cake. Remove and cut all dowels evenly to the highest pencil mark. Plastic dowels cut very easily; just score with a knife then snap to make a clean break. Push the dowels back down into the cake until level with the surface.

Applying sugarpaste around sides

5 To cover the cake, first moisten around the top edge with edible glue. Roll out the remaining white sugarpaste and cut a piece around 50cm (20in) in length and measuring the height of the cake plus 1cm (½in). Sprinkle the surface of the sugarpaste with a little icing sugar to prevent sticking and then gently roll up into a spiral. This helps the sugarpaste keep its shape when being applied. Place the rolled up sugarpaste against the side of the cake and unroll around it **(see above)**. Trim excess away from the join and secure the join closed with a little edible glue. To remove the join completely, smooth gently with a little icing sugar on your fingertips.

6 Indent a ring around the centre of the waste bin by pressing the flat edge of a ruler against it. Scratch lines over the surface with a knife, using the ruler as a guide. Position the cake card on top of the cake to help support the modelled pieces later.

7 To make the alarm clock, roll 175g (6oz) of pale grey modelling paste into a ball and press down with a cake smoother to make a flattened circle 8cm (3¼in) diameter. Press the 6cm (2½in) circle cutter into the surface to indent a ring for the clock face. Thinly roll out 10g (¼oz) of white modelling paste and cut a circle for the clock face. Repeat cutting another circle using pale grey for the back of the alarm clock.

8 To make the clock feet, split 15g (½oz) of pale grey in half and roll into oval shapes, sticking each in place on the base of the clock. Press down on the work surface to flatten the bottom of each. Stick a tiny flattened circle onto the centre of the clock face. Using the black royal icing and the no.1 plain piping tube, pipe the numbers around the clock face. Start by piping 12, 3, 6 and 9, and then fill in with the smaller numbers. Pipe the large and small clock face hands **(see below)**.

9 For the alarm clock spring, roll 5g (just under ¼oz) of white modelling paste into a thin even sausage and wrap around a length of dowelling. Set aside to dry. Stick two flattened circles of pale grey onto the top of the alarm to make the alarm buttons. Split the remainder in half and shape into dome shapes for the bells, sticking a tiny flattened circle onto the top of each. Stick one bell in place and set aside the other. Make a small hole into the top of the alarm clock using a cocktail stick ready for the spring.

10 Thinly roll out the remaining white modelling paste and cut 6–7 sheets of 'paper', each sheet measuring around 20 x 13cm (12 x 8in). Lay some into the top of the waste bin and crumple up others. Stick the alarm clock in position on top of the cake at a slight angle and stick papers around the base to help hold it in place.

Piping clock face numerals with royal icing

11 To make the telephone receiver, roll 115g (4oz) of ivory modelling paste into a fat sausage and then roll at the central part only, rocking backwards and forwards until the two ends are rounded off. Press down to flatten each end slightly. Mark lines for the earpiece using the tip of a knife and then indent the mouthpiece using a bone or ball tool, indenting three holes using the tip of a cocktail stick. Set aside to dry.

12 With the remaining ivory modelling paste, indent into the centre of a pea sized ball and stick in place at the mouthpiece end. Roll the remainder into a long thin sausage and spiral around the dowelling to make the spring **(see above right)**. Leave to set for a few moments, and then stick in place in the waste bin with the telephone receiver against the side supported by the blue file, securing with a dab of white royal icing. Use pieces of foam to support in position until dry.

13 Roll out the remaining red modelling paste and cut out the tie, smoothing around the cut edge to soften. Stick in position draped over the waste bin and down the side. Model three flattened circles from blue modelling paste trimmings and stick in place. To finish, push the spring into the top of the alarm clock securing with a little edible glue, and stick the broken alarm bell at the front resting on the papers.

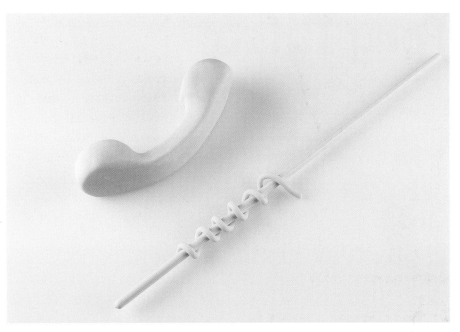

Loop paste around dowelling to make spring coil wire

The crumpled 'paper' helps to hold the heavier pieces in position

Pony Palace

Even ponies can be princesses can't they? My little girl thinks so.
Make her birthday extra special with a beautiful palace birthday cake
fit for any princess.

What you will need

See page 7–11 for all recipes and baking chart

- 1 x 20cm (8in) and 10cm (4in) round sponge cakes
- 35cm (14in) round cake board
- 10cm (4in) round cake card
- Icing (powdered) sugar in a sugar shaker

Sugarpaste
- 1.25kg (2lb 12oz) dark lilac
- 315g (11oz) lilac
- 45g (1½oz) dark grey

Modelling paste
- 285g (10oz) pale lilac
- Tiny piece of black
- 30g (1oz) brown
- 50g (1¾oz) cream
- 20g (¾oz) pale grey
- 30g (1oz) yellow

Royal icing
10g (¼oz) lilac

- 600g (1lb 5¼oz / 2½c) buttercream
- Edible glue and brush
- Pink powder food colouring

Equipment
- Cake layer cutter
- Large rolling pin
- Small plain bladed knife
- Serrated carving knife
- 4 x food safe dowelling
- Ruler
- Cake smoother
- A few cocktail sticks
- 4cm (1½in) and 5cm (2in) oval shaped cutters
- Bone or ball tool
- No.3 and no.18 plain piping tubes (PME)
- Foam pieces
- No.6 sable paintbrush

Tip
Short of time? You could replace the sugar model with a non-toxic, food-safe toy, which can be removed before serving and kept as a gift.

1 Knead 500g (1lb 1¾oz) of dark lilac sugarpaste until soft and pliable. Roll out with a sprinkling of icing sugar to prevent sticking and cover the cake board. Rub the surface with a cake smoother and then trim excess from around the edge. Set aside to dry.

2 Trim the crust from both cakes and level the tops. Cut two layers in each cake and sandwich back together with buttercream. Spread the underside of both cakes with buttercream and position the large cake centrally on the cake board and the smaller cake on the cake card.

3 Using a ruler, measure the height of the larger cake. Roll out 450g (1lb) of dark lilac sugarpaste and cut a strip measuring 60cm (25in) length x the height of the cake. Dust with icing sugar to prevent sticking and then roll up from one end. Lift and place against the front of the cake and unroll around it **(see below)**. Trim excess at join and smooth closed. Use a cake smoother to gain a smooth surface.

4 Roll out the remaining dark lilac and cover the top of the cake, trimming excess and keeping a neat edge. Cover the smaller cake in the same way using the lilac sugarpaste. Push the three dowels down into the large cake keeping them well spaced but no wider than the base of the smaller cake. Mark each level with the top of the cake, remove and then trim to the highest measurement of all three dowels. Push the dowels back into the cake and then place the smaller cake on top, securing around the edge with a little edible glue.

Unroll the sugarpaste around the cake sides

5 To make the roof tower, roll 125g (4½oz) of pale lilac modelling paste into a sausage and leave to set for a few moments before re-rolling to prevent the back flattening. Use the bone or ball tool to indent the window, moving the tool up and down to indent a small oval window. When the tower has set, push a dowel into the bottom to make a hole, pushing gently until it comes through at the top. Remove the dowel and then position the tower upright and leave to dry completely.

6 To make the roof shape, roll 75g (2½oz) of pale lilac modelling paste into a teardrop shape and hollow out the base slightly by pinching an edge. Check that the roof fits onto the tower and then remove and leave to dry separately.

7 Cut out the stable door at the front of the cake measuring 10cm (4in) width, cutting a slight curve into the top. Remove the sugarpaste and use this as a template for the dark grey shadow effect. Cut out all the windows using the larger oval cutter for the base cake's three windows and the smaller cutter for the two windows on the second tier. Thinly roll out the dark grey sugarpaste and cut pieces to fill the door area and windows, smoothing the joins closed and sticking around the outside edge with a little edible glue.

8 For the stable door, roll out the brown modelling paste and cut a strip 4cm (1½in) height and measuring slightly less than the width of the door opening. Indent into the centre using the edge of the ruler. Indent again into each half, pushing in with less pressure and then again, making a total of four planks on each half. Mark wood grain using a knife. Stick the stable door in place taking care not to disturb the straight lines.

9 To make the door handles, roll out a little pale grey modelling paste and cut two circles using the larger piping tube tip. Cut out a circle from the centre of each using the smaller tube. Use this smaller circle for the bolt at the top of each. Cut eight more small circles for the door hinges. To make the pebble effect pavement, model different sized oval shapes using the remaining pale grey and stick in position over the cake board, pressing flat and grouping them around the stable entrance.

10 To make the pony's body, roll 25g (just over ¾oz) of cream modelling paste into a long teardrop and bend the narrow end gently upwards to curve the pony's back. Set aside to dry flat. To make the legs, split 10g (¼oz) of cream into four pieces. To make a leg, roll a sausage rounding off one end for the thigh. Pinch gently at the bottom to round off the hoof. Bend the leg by pinching out and pushing in at the back. Stick in position on the pony's body **(see left)**.

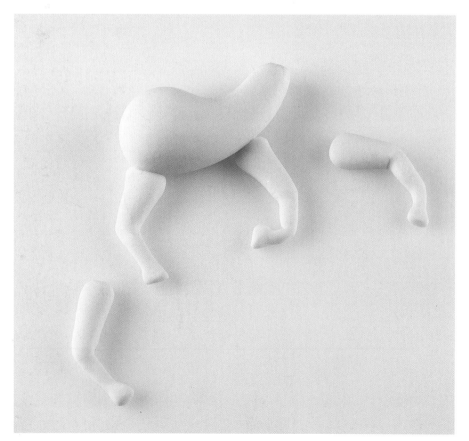

Stick the legs in position with edible glue

11 For the saddle, roll an oval shape using just under 5g (¼oz) of pale lilac modelling paste and press flat, smoothing down around the edge. Stick in position on the pony's back edged with tiny circles cut from the no.3 piping tube.

Cutting circles for the roof tiles

paintbrush. For ears, shape tiny teardrops and indent into the centre of each using the end of a paintbrush. Stick in position with the point upwards. Roll a tiny ball of cream, press flat and cut in half for eyelids. For eyes, roll two tiny ball pupils and edge each with a tiny tapering sausage for eyelashes. When the pony is dry, stick in position against the castle with royal icing. Wedge a foam piece underneath the pony to hold in place whilst drying; this will stop the figure sinking, which could cause damage to the legs. With the yellow modelling paste, shape different sized tapering sausages for the mane and tail, building up little by little and curling and flicking the ends. Secure each one with a little edible glue **(see right)**.

Head shape step-by-step

14 Dust a little pink powder colouring onto the pony's cheeks and saddle and then dust colour around the base of the cake and over the top of the roof.

12 Thinly roll out the remaining pale lilac modelling paste and cut all the circles to edge the top of each tier, stable door and window trims **(see above)**. Assemble the tower in position with the dowelling for support and secure at the base with a little edible glue. Stick the roof on top and then cover the roof with circular tiles, overlapping each layer. Make the finial using two small ball shapes, the smaller on top.

13 To make the pony's head, roll 10g (¼oz) of cream into a ball and pinch along one third to gently round off and lengthen the muzzle. Indent the smile using the wide end of a piping tube and dimple the corners using a cocktail stick. Mark nostrils by pushing in with the end of a

Add circles to edge the top of each cake and use for roof tiles

Pot of Gold

We all dream of a pot of gold at the end of the rainbow, so now you can make your own. Perhaps it will even bring you or the recipient some good luck...

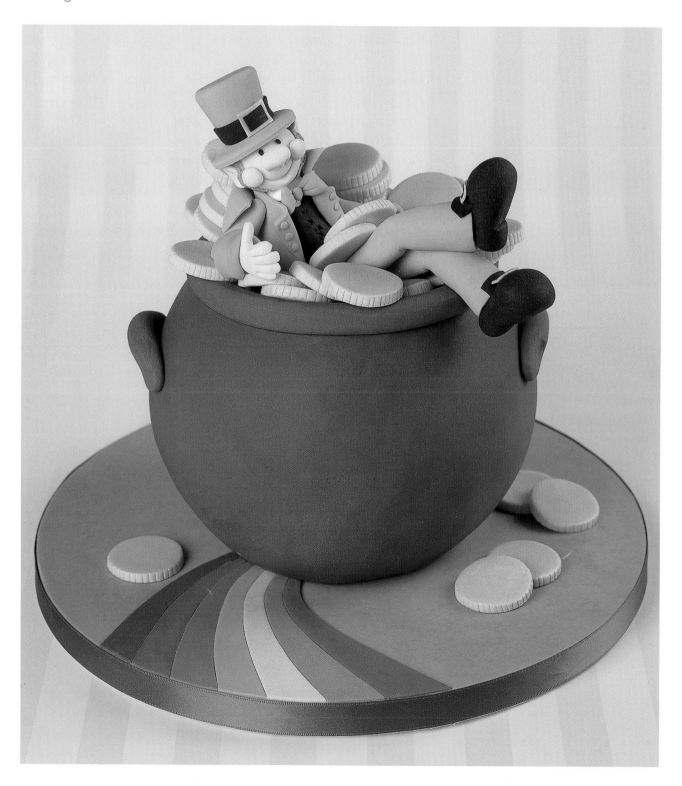

What you will need

See page 7–11 for all recipes and baking chart

- 1 x 20cm (8in) round sponge cake
- 1 x 2L (4 pint) bowl-shaped sponge cake
- 30cm (12in) round cake board
- Icing (powdered) sugar in a sugar shaker

Sugarpaste
- 450g (1lb) green
- 60g (2oz) black
- 770g (1lb 11oz) dark grey

Modelling paste
- 10g (¼oz) purple
- 10g (¼oz) mauve
- 10g (¼oz) blue
- 145g (5oz) green
- 340g (12oz) yellow
- 10g (¼oz) orange
- 10g (14oz) red
- 45g (1½oz) black
- 45g (1½oz) white
- 30g (1oz) flesh
- 5g (just under ¼oz) golden brown

- Green food colouring paste
- 1 Tbsp cool, boiled water
- 500g (1lb 1¾oz / 2¼c) buttercream
- Edible gold lustre powder
- Sugar stick or length of raw, dried spaghetti
- Edible glue and brush

Equipment
- Large rolling pin
- Cake smoother
- Plain bladed cutting knife
- No.6 sable paintbrush
- Serrated knife
- Cake layer cutter
- Foam pieces (for support)
- No.1 (PME) plain piping tube (tip)
- 1.5 (⅝in), 3.5cm (1¼in) and 4cm (1½in) circle cutters
- New food-safe scourer (for texture)

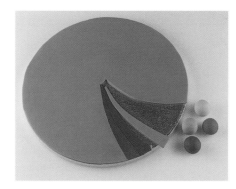

Cut tapering strips for rainbow

1 Knead the green sugarpaste until soft and pliable. Roll out using a sprinkling of icing sugar to prevent sticking and cover the board. Trim excess from around the edge and smooth the surface with a cake smoother. Cut out a strip 17cm (6½in) width along the edge of the cake board, curving it into the centre. Using the rainbow colours, roll out and cut tapering strips to fill the space **(see above)**. For a grass effect, dilute green food colouring with a little water and stipple colour over the green covering on the cake board and set aside to dry.

2 Trim the crust from each cake and slice the tops flat. Sandwich the round cake on top of the bowl-shaped cake and trim a little around the top edge to round off. Cut a layer in each cake using the layer cutter and sandwich all layers together with buttercream. Spread a layer over the surface of the cake as a crumb coat to seal the cake and help the sugarpaste stick.

3 Thinly roll out the black sugarpaste and cut a piece to cover the top of the cake, trimming neatly around the edge. Roll out the dark grey sugarpaste and cut a strip the height of the cake measuring at least 55cm (22in). Sprinkle with icing sugar to prevent sticking and then roll up from one end. Lift and position against the side of the cake and unroll the covering around it, trimming excess from the join and smoothing closed **(see below)**. Rub the surface with a cake smoother and position the cake centrally on the cake board.

Unroll sugarpaste around cake sides

4 Roll a sausage with dark grey trimmings to make the rim of the pot, and two small sausages for handles, securing all with a little edible glue. Make 35–40 coins next using the yellow modelling paste and the medium sized circle cutter. As each is cut, press the back of a knife around the edge for the grip lines. Rub gold lustre powder over the surface using your fingertips and then set aside to dry. Alternatively, you can use gold foil-covered chocolate coins for the gold treasure instead.

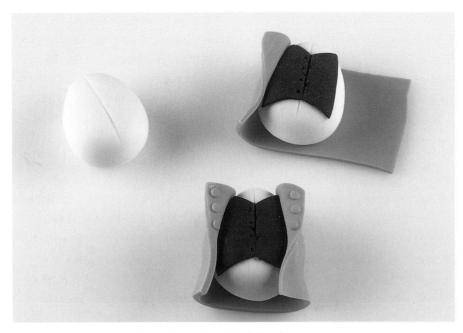

Wrap the jacket around the body and turn back lapels

measuring 5 x 10cm (2 x 4in). Wrap around the body sticking with edible glue and then turn back the top two corners making the lapels. Roll six tiny ball buttons to edge each lapel **(see left)**. Stick the body into the top of the pot and build up gold coins to support the figure.

9 Roll the remaining white into a ball, press flat and then cut a small 'v' from the front making the shirt collar. To make the arms, split 20g (½oz) of green modelling paste in half and roll into tapering sausage shapes. Press to flatten the full end of each sleeve and bend halfway to shape the elbow. Stick in position supported by coins.

5 To make the figure, make the trousers first by splitting 60g (2oz) of green modelling paste in half and rolling each into long tapering sausages. Press the rounded end of each trouser flat and bend half way for the knee. Stick in position using a little edible glue, supported with a piece of foam until dry.

6 For shoes, split 30g (1oz) of black modelling paste in half and roll into teardrop shapes. Press down on the point of each to round off for the heel. Push the flat of a knife against the bottom of each sole to indent the heels. Roll out and cut a small square for each shoe flap and stick in position with the shoes using foam pieces for support if necessary.

7 Set aside 5g (just under ¼oz) of white modelling paste for the collar later and then roll the remainder into a rounded teardrop for the shirt.

Mark a line down the centre using a knife. Thinly roll out black for the waistcoat cutting out the shape using the template (see page 127). Mark a line down the centre and mark pleats with the tip of a knife. Indent buttons by pushing in with the no.1 plain piping tube.

8 To make the jacket, thinly roll out 25g (just over ½oz) of green modelling paste and cut a strip

10 Push the sugar stick down through the body until a little is protruding to help hold the head in place. To make the head, roll 20g (½oz) of flesh modelling paste into a ball and flatten the facial area slightly. To mark the smile, push the small circle cutter into the mouth area at an upwards angle and then using a damp glue brush stroke the bottom lip down

Face detailing

at the centre. Stick an oval shaped nose onto the centre and indent nostrils by pushing in with the end of a paintbrush. Stick two pea-sized ball cheeks either side. For ears, roll two teardrop shapes and indent into the centre of each using the end of a paintbrush. Stick in position with points upwards, bending each out a little at the top **(see below left)**. Roll two tiny ball shaped black eyes. For hair, roll out the golden brown modelling paste and texture by pressing firmly over the surface with the scourer. Tear the textured paste into small pieces and build up around his face and the sides of his head only, leaving the top bare.

11 To make hands, split the remaining flesh in half and roll into teardrop shapes. Make a cut into the rounded end on one side for the thumb, cutting down no more than halfway. Make three slightly shorter cuts along the top to separate fingers. Stroke gently to remove ridges and round off the tips and then stick in position against the end of each sleeve. For cuffs, split 10g (¼oz) of green modelling paste in half and roll into fat sausages. Press each flat and mark twice to indent pleats. Stick in place wrapped around the bottom of each sleeve, holding the hands in place securely.

12 Make the collar and bow tie next using 5g (just under ¼oz) of green modelling paste. First roll out and cut a strip measuring 6cm (2½in) in length and slice at an angle either end to create a pointed collar. Stick in position around his neck with the points uppermost and turned out slightly. For the bow, shape two small teardrop shapes, press flat and cut the rounded end of each straight. Mark pleats with the tip of a knife. Stick onto the front of the shirt with a small ball of green at the centre.

13 For the hat brim, thinly roll out green modelling paste and cut a circle using the largest circle cutter and stick in position on top of his head. Roll the remainder into a teardrop shape and press down on the full end to flatten for the top of the

hat. Press down on the point and then place on its side and roll to straighten. Stick in position and then thinly roll out the remaining black modelling paste and cut a strip for the hatband.

14 Thinly roll out yellow trimmings and cut three squares, one large for the hat buckle and two small for the shoe buckles. Thinly roll out black trimmings and cover the centre of each buckle with slightly smaller squares. Stack some more coins into the pot and scatter over the cake board.

Side view

Circus Train

Here's a fun cake for younger children complete with a cute clown leading the way and simply shaped circus animals filling the windows of brightly decorated carriages.

What you will need

See page 7–11 for all recipes and baking chart

- 25 x 15cm (10 x 6in) oblong shaped sponge cake
- 20 x 30cm (8 x 12in) oblong shaped cake board
- Icing (powdered) sugar in a sugar shaker

Sugarpaste
- 450g (1lb) lime green
- 340g (12oz) blue
- 315g (11oz) red
- 400g (14oz) yellow

Modelling paste
- 115g (4oz) yellow
- 20g (¾oz) blue
- 90g (3oz) black
- 60g (2oz) red
- 45g (1½oz) pale grey
- 10g (¼oz) white
- 20g (¾oz) pale brown
- 10g (¼oz) pink
- 30g (1oz) pale egg yellow
- 90g (3oz) golden brown
- 30g (1oz) dark brown
- 20g (¾oz) flesh

- 450g (1lb / 2c) buttercream
- Edible glue and brush
- Sugar stick or length of raw, dried spaghetti

Equipment
- Cake layer cutter
- Large rolling pin
- Small plain bladed knife
- Serrated carving knife
- Cake smoother
- A few cocktail sticks
- 3cm (1¼in) and 4cm (1½in) square cutters
- No.3 plain piping tube
- Ruler
- 2.5cm (1in) and 3cm (1¼in) circle cutters
- Foam pieces
- Scissors

Tip

If more servings are required you can lengthen the train by making more carriages on another oblong cake board and present them together.

1 Knead the lime green sugarpaste until soft and pliable. Roll out with a sprinkling of icing sugar to prevent sticking and cover the cake board. Rub the surface with a cake smoother and then trim excess from around the edge. Set aside to dry.

Fill layers with buttercream

2 Trim the crust from the cake and level the top. To make the engine, cut a 10cm (4in) strip from one end of the cake. Cut this strip in half widthways and then stack one on top of the other. Trim opposite ends to taper slightly towards the base. To give extra height to the engine, cut two more layers in the cake using the layer cutter. Cut the pointed roof, cutting down to the second layer. Sandwich all four layers together with buttercream and then spread a thin layer over the surface as a crumb coat to seal the cake and to help the sugarpaste stick **(see above)**.

3 To make the train carriage, cut the remaining cake in half and position one on top of the other making an oblong shaped carriage. Check that the two cakes sit together neatly and re-trim if necessary. Sandwich the layer together with buttercream and then spread a layer over the surface as before.

Use a cake smoother to flatten out any imperfections

4 To cover the engine, first re-work the buttercream on the front of the engine to soften the surface. Roll out blue sugarpaste and place the front of the engine down onto it. Cut around the shape keeping a neat even edge. Cover the back of the engine in the same way, then the two opposite sides securing joins with a little edible glue. Press gently over the surface with a cake smoother **(see above)**.

5 For the engine base at the front, roll out the remaining blue sugarpaste 2cm (1in) thickness and cut an oblong measuring 7 x 3.5cm (2¾ x 1½in). Position the engine on the cake board at a slight angle with the engine base.

6 For the roof, roll out 145g (5oz) of red sugarpaste and cut a piece to cover the top of the engine. If the paste stretches and becomes misshapen, press along the edge with a ruler or cake smoother, or re-trim if necessary by using the hard surface to cut against.

7 Cut out two windows either side using the 3cm (1¼in) square cutter and two circular holes at the front using the wide end of the piping tube. Thinly roll out black modelling paste and fill each window, using a little edible glue to secure around the outside edges.

8 Roll 60g (2oz) of red sugarpaste into a fat sausage and cut one end straight. Stick this in position on top of the engine base. Roll a small ball of yellow modelling paste, press flat and then indent into the top using the bone or ball tool. Stick this in place on top of the engine.

9 For the funnel, roll 10g (¼oz) of blue modelling paste into a sausage rounding off one end. Indent into the rounded end with the bone or ball tool. Leave to set for a few moments placed upside down on the fuller end before sticking in position.

10 Model two small, flattened circles of red modelling paste for the bumper supports and make slightly larger flattened circles for the bumpers. Stick a tiny ball of blue onto the front of the engine.

11 Cover the carriage cake in the same way as the engine using yellow sugarpaste for the sides and the remaining red for the flat roof. Cut and fill windows as before using the 4cm (1½in) square cutter, also cutting a window at the front and back. Cut out a small hole in the top of the carriage using the 3cm (1¼in) circle cutter for the giraffe. Position the cake on the cake board.

12 For the wheels, split 30g (1oz) each of red and yellow modelling paste into 12 pieces, two slightly smaller than the others for the smaller front engine wheels. To make a wheel, knead a piece each of red and yellow modelling paste together until streaky. Roll into a long sausage measuring 10cm (4in) and then roll into a spiral. Make all the wheels and stick in place with a little edible glue.

13 Thinly roll out blue modelling paste and cut a strip to join the engine to the carriage. For the red bolts, cut two oblong shapes sticking in place just above the blue strip and attach two tiny circular bolts on each cut from the no.3 plain piping tube. Thickly roll out red modelling paste and cut strips for the window ledges. Cut two long thin strips of red to edge along the top of each side of the carriage.

14 Thinly roll out yellow modelling paste and cut out circles using the circle cutters. Cut the circles in half and use to edge along the top of both the engine and carriage on both sides.

15
MONKEY

Moisten the monkey's window area with a little edible glue and allow for the surface to dry a little and become tacky. To make the monkey's head, roll a 15g (½oz) ball of pale brown modelling paste and slice a little from the back to make a flat surface and then stick in place supported by the window ledge. Using pink, model flattened circles for muzzle and ears. Indent the smile using the wide end of the piping tube and mark a line down the centre of the muzzle using a knife. Dimple the corners of the mouth with a cocktail stick. Indent each ear using the bone or ball tool. Roll a small oval-shaped pink nose and roll the remaining pink into a sausage shaped tail. Model two tiny black eyes.

ELEPHANT

Using the grey modelling paste, make the elephant's head, gently twisting and pinching out his trunk and curling up slightly. Cut a slice at the back as before and stick in place at the front window. Model two flattened teardrop shaped ears from the trimmings and make two tiny black eyes. Indent a hole either side of the trunk using the end of the paintbrush and stick a white teardrop shaped tusk into each, smoothing the tips up slightly and pointing them outwards.

TIGER

Roll a 45g (1½oz) ball of golden brown modelling paste and slice a little from the back as before. For ears, roll two small ball shapes and indent into each using the bone or ball tool. Model two teardrop shapes for the muzzle using the trimmings, indenting whisker holes using the tip of a cocktail stick. Build up teardrop shapes for his mane. Make two tiny black eyes and a nose.

BROWN BEAR

Make the bear's head and ears as before using the dark brown modelling paste. Model a ball shaped muzzle indented in the centre. For the open mouth, push in the end of the paintbrush and move gently up and down, pulling out a tiny bottom lip.

GIRAFFE

Roll the egg yellow modelling paste into a fat sausage and then pinch gently one third of the length to narrow the neck area and round off the head. Roll the eye area to narrow and round off the muzzle. Indent the smile with the wide end of the piping tube and dimple the corners with a cocktail stick. For nostrils, push in either side with the end of a paintbrush. Cut across the

bottom of his neck to create a straight base so the figure will sit straight in the opening later. Using trimmings, roll two tiny sausages for horns rounding off the top of each and shape two flattened teardrops for ears **(see below)**. Roll a tiny ball, press flat and then cut in half and use for eyelids. Roll two tiny black eyes and two minute sausages to edge the top of each for eyelashes. Stick tiny flattened misshapen patches of pale brown over his back. For the mane, roll a long sausage of pale brown, press flat and then make angular cuts down either side using scissors. Stick the giraffe's head in position in the hole at the top of the carriage. If necessary, use foam pieces for support whilst drying.

The back of the carriage has an animal bottom and tail. Roll 30g (1oz) of golden brown modelling paste into a ball and indent a line using a knife. Cut excess at the back as before and stick in place at the back window. To

make the tail, roll the remaining golden brown into a long sausage and round off one end. Pinch this end to a point and then make cuts for the hair.

16
CLOWN

For the trousers, roll 45g (1½oz) of yellow modelling paste into a fat teardrop shape and cut halfway down on the narrow end to separate legs. Pinch each leg to open and narrow each and then smooth the cut lines by rubbing gently with your fingertips. Pinch around the top of the rounded end to widen and stick in place on top of the engine roof.

To make the clown's top, flatten a 15g (½oz) ball of red modelling paste and make a cut either side for sleeves. Push into the bottom of each sleeve to make a small hole for the arms later. Smooth around the shape to remove the hard edge and stick in position on the trousers ensuring the trousers are much wider than the base of the body.

To make the boots, split 15g (½oz) of black modelling paste in half. Roll each into oval shapes and indent the heels by pressing in with the flat of a knife. Stick in position at the base of the trousers.

With the remaining blue modelling paste model a flattened circle for a collar, roll out and cut two strips for the braces, both tapering wider at one end and stick in position crossed over at the back. Roll sausages and indent pleats in the centre of each and use for turn-ups to edge the base of the trousers and at the end of each sleeve.

Push the sugar stick or length of spaghetti down through the collar and body until 1cm (¼in) is protruding.

Giraffe's head step-by-step

Roll 15g (½oz) of flesh modelling paste into a ball for his head. To make his mouth, roll a pea-sized amount of white into a sausage and press flat, curving the two ends upwards into a smile. Stick in position on the clown's face and indent using the wide end of the piping tube. Dimple the corners using a cocktail stick. Roll another pea-sized amount of white into a shorter sausage, press flat and then cut in half to make the eyes. Stick in place with a small oval shaped black pupil on each. For ears, roll two small ball shapes and indent into the centre of each using the end of a paintbrush. Stick a red ball nose onto the centre of his face. Push the clown's head gently down onto the sugar stick securing at the collar with a little edible glue. For hair, roll a sausage using the orange modelling paste and pinch along the length and stick in place with each end resting on the top of each ear **(see above)**.

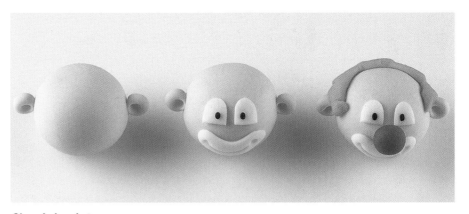

Clown's head stages

18 Thinly roll out the remaining red and leave to firm but not harden and dry completely. Repeatedly press the piping tube tip over the surface to cut all the circles to decorate the clown's trousers, using four for the buttons on the braces. Tip them out of the tube and then pick them up, one by one with the glue brush damp with glue and stick in position.

17 Split the remaining flesh modelling paste in half and make two short sausage shaped arms. To make the gloves, first stick a pea-sized amount of white modelling paste onto the end of each arm and then split the remainder in half. To make the hand, roll into a teardrop shape and press down to flatten a little. Make a small cut no further than half way for the thumb and then three short cuts across the top for fingers. Smooth around the shape to round off the tips and push the thumb down towards the palm. Make the opposite hand and stick both in position resting against the trousers.

Back view of cake

Wash Day

Take an amusing look at everyday life, with piles and piles of washing and a fun figure showing her underwear lodged into the washing machine opening.

What you will need

See page 7–11 for all recipes and baking chart

- 25cm (10in) square sponge cake
- 30cm (12in) round cake board
- Icing (powdered) sugar in a sugar shaker

Sugarpaste
- 1.25kg (2lb 12oz) white
- 60g (2oz) pale blue

Modelling paste
- 15g (½oz) black
- 115g (4oz) white
- 10g (¼oz) pale grey
- 30g (1oz) flesh
- 90g (3oz) turquoise
- 15g (½oz) dark blue
- 45g (1½oz) red
- 90g (3oz) green
- 115g (4oz) pale blue
- 90g (3oz) blue
- 60g (2oz) purple
- 45g (1½oz) orange
- 15g (½oz) pink

Royal icing
- 15g (½oz / 2¾c) white

- 550g (1lb 3½oz / 2¾c) buttercream
- Edible glue and brush
- Edible silver lustre powder
- A few drops clear alcohol (vodka, gin)

Equipment
- Large rolling pin
- Small plain bladed knife
- Serrated carving knife
- Ruler
- Cake smoother
- 6cm (2¼in) shallow bowl (Arcoroc)
- A few cocktail sticks
- Foam sheet
- Foam pieces (for support whilst drying)
- No.6 sable paintbrush
- No.4 plain piping tube
- Bone or ball tool
- Large blossom plunger cutter
- New food safe scourer

> ### Tip
> If you do not have the particular bowl to make the washing machine door, simply cut an 8cm (3in) circle of white modelling paste instead and place into the base of any size bowl to dry.

1 Knead 340g (12oz) of white and the pale blue sugarpaste separately until both are soft and pliable and then knead together until streaky. For the swirl effect cake board covering, roll the streaky sugarpaste into a long sausage and then spiral into a circle **(see below)**. Press down on the surface and then roll out with a sprinkling of

icing sugar to prevent sticking and cover the cake board. Rub the surface with a cake smoother and then trim excess from around the edge. Set aside to dry.

2 Trim the crust from the cake and level the top. Cut the cake exactly in half and then half again to make four equal squares. Stack one on top of the other and re-trim if necessary to keep the sides completely smooth and level. Sandwich all three layers together with buttercream and then spread a thin layer over the surface as a crumb coat to seal the cake and to help the sugarpaste stick.

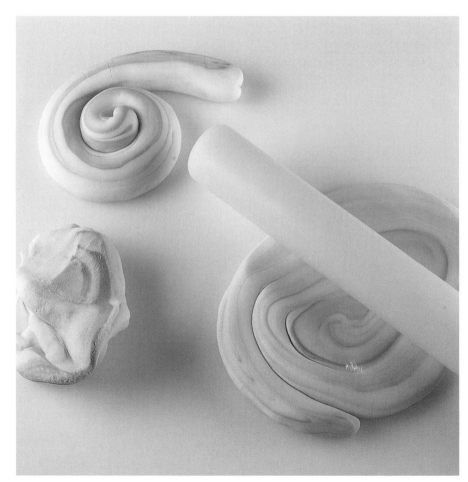

Roll out the spiral of paste to make the 'swirl' effect cake board covering

3 Re-work the buttercream if it has set or spread on a little more. Roll out 185g (6½oz) of white sugarpaste and place one side of the cake down onto it and cut around, keeping the cut neat. Cover the opposite side in the same way. Spread a little buttercream on the underside of the cake and then position upright on the centre of the cake board. Rub the covered surfaces with a cake smoother to remove dimples and create a smooth surface.

4 Using a ruler to measure, roll out 185g (6½oz) of white sugarpaste and cut a piece to fit the back of the cake; covering this way will prevent the sides already covered being damaged **(see below)**. Cover the front next, using a further 185g (6½oz), smoothing all joins closed and securing with a little edible glue. With the remaining white, roll out and cover the top of the cake. Stick the join closed and then run the knife along it to make a feature.

5 To mark more detailing on the front, press down with the edge of the ruler to indent a line along the bottom and again for the control panel at the top. Indent another line to mark the drawer. Use the end of a paintbrush to indent the drawer handle by moving it backwards and forwards rounding off each end. Cut out a hole in the front for the drum using the

6cm (2¼in) circle cutter, removing the sugarpaste. Thinly roll out black modelling paste and cut a circle to fill the space.

6 Dust the small bowl with a little icing sugar. To make the drum door, thinly roll out 30g (1oz) of white modelling paste and push gently into the small bowl, smoothing around the inside to shape the contours and then cut neatly around the outside edge. Make sure the paste is loose and keep moving slightly whilst drying to prevent sticking to the inside of the bowl. When the door has set, remove from the bowl and place on a foam sheet to dry completely.

Use a ruler to cut sizes correctly

7 Thinly roll out pale grey modelling paste and cut two thin strips, one to edge around the drum and the other for the door seal. Mix a little edible silver lustre powder with a few drops of clear alcohol and paint a spiralled glass effect on the door using the no.6 paintbrush.

8 Stick two pea-sized flattened circles of white modelling paste on the front for the controls, indenting into the centre of each with the small end of a bone or ball tool. Fill with a tiny sausage of pale grey modelling paste. Thinly roll out white modelling paste and cut five circles using the no.4 plain piping tube (tip) and stick in a line for the buttons.

9 To make the legs, split the flesh modelling paste in half. Roll one into a sausage and bend one end round for the foot. Pinch to narrow the ankle and round off the foot. Push in underneath the foot to indent the arch. Bend the leg half way by pinching the knee then pushing in gently at the back **(see above)**. Make the second leg and set both aside.

10 For slippers, split 10g (⅓oz) of turquoise modelling paste into four pieces. Roll two into sausage shapes for the soles indenting into the centre of each to narrow and then press each flat. Stick in position on the bottom of each foot. For the top of each slipper, roll the remaining two pieces into sausages and texture by pressing down onto the scourer and then stick in position over each foot and joining the sole either side.

Leg step-by-step

11 Thinly roll out the dark blue modelling paste, gather up and stick in place spilling out of the drum. For the knickers, roll a ball using 45g (1½oz) of white modelling paste and indent to mark the centre using a cocktail stick. Pinch around the bottom of the knickers to frill each leg and then indent a line just above the frill using a cocktail stick.

12 Assemble the knickers, legs and slippers against the cake securing with edible glue. If necessary, use foam pieces for support whilst drying. Knead 5g (just under ¼oz) each of red and blue together until streaky. Roll out and cut a strip for the clothing edging the knickers. Thinly roll out and cut circles of red using the tip of the no.4 piping tube and use for the polka-dot pattern on the knickers.

13 Using the coloured sugarpaste, make all the remaining clothing, kneading different quantities of blues, greens and purple together to make all the different shades. Most of the clothing piles are thinly rolled out paste gathered up into pleats and folds. For texture, use the scourer and the back of a knife to indent lines for a tartan or striped effect. The floral pattern is made by first rolling out purple modelling paste and then rolling blue paste extremely thin. Cut blossom flowers from this paste and stick over the surface of the purple, along with red circles for the centres cut from the piping tube. Roll the surface with a rolling pin to indent the pattern, moving the paste frequently whilst rolling to prevent sticking.

14 For the trousers, roll 60g (2oz) of modelling paste into a sausage, press flat and then cut three quarters down from the top to separate legs. Smooth to remove edges and indent detailing with a knife **(see below)**.

Simply modelled clothing

15 To make a pair of socks, split 10g (¼oz) of modelling paste in half and roll into sausages bending half way. Press down on the foot and to open the top, push in with the end of a paintbrush. Mark the ribbing using the tip of a knife. With red and green, cut two small buttons for the machine using the piping tube.

16 To make the detergent box, cut out an oblong shape using white modelling paste. For the flaps, thinly roll out modelling paste and cut strips the length and width of the box and stick upright onto the top edges of the box. As the flaps dry, stroke them down slightly taking care not to push too much or they may fall. Fill the box with icing sugar for the 'detergent'. Roll a thin sausage of turquoise and spiral round for the box detailing.

17 For the conditioner bottle, first put aside a pea sized amount of pink modelling paste. Roll the remainder into an oval shape and pinch gently around one end to narrow the neck of the bottle. Push in with the end of a paintbrush to open up. Roll gently to narrow the base and then stick in place with two teardrop shaped drips and a flattened piece spread out level with the board covering for the spill. Using the remaining pale grey, stick flattened circles onto the front of the conditioner bottle cut from the piping tube and roll a teardrop shape for the lid, pressing down on the full end to flatten. Mark the grip lines using a knife and indent the top using the piping tube.

18 When the door is dry, stick in position against the front of the cake level with the drum using a dab of royal icing to secure. To prevent the door slipping, use a foam piece to support underneath.

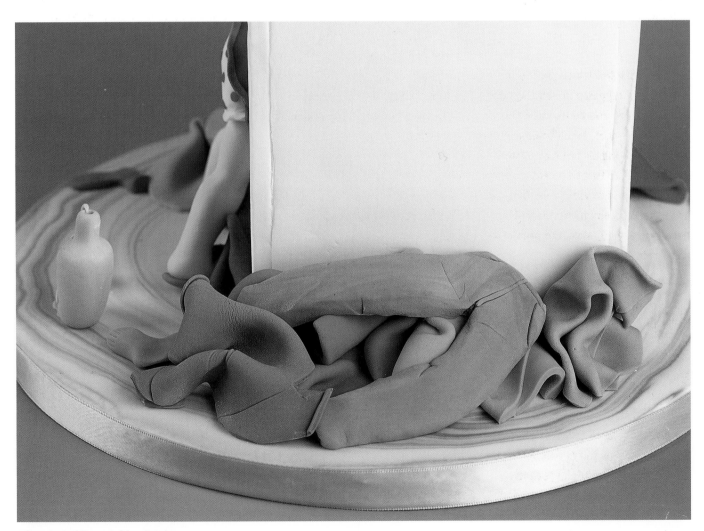

Pile of clothing at side of cake

Pampered Pet

Appealing to young and old alike, here's an extremely quick and simple design of a cute kitten lounging on her comfy cushion bed.

What you will need

See page 7–11 for all recipes and baking chart

- 25cm (10in) round sponge cake
- 35cm (14in) round cake board
- Icing (powdered) sugar in a sugar shaker

Sugarpaste
- 500g (1lb 1¾oz) pink
- 1kg (2lb 3¼oz) lilac
- 270g (9½oz) white
- 15g (½oz) pink
- Tiny piece of black

- 550g (1lb 3½oz / 2¾c) buttercream
- Edible glue and glue brush

Equipment
- Large rolling pin
- Small plain bladed knife
- Serrated carving knife
- Cake layer cutter
- Cake smoother
- A few cocktail sticks
- New food-safe scourer
- Miniature circle cutter
- 6 black stamens

Note

Although the stamens used for the kitten's whiskers are food-safe, please remember to remove before serving as they are inedible.

1 Knead the pink sugarpaste until soft and pliable. Roll out using a sprinkling of icing sugar to prevent sticking and cover the cake board. Roll the rolling pin over the surface pressing gently to indent ripples. Trim excess from around the edge and reserve trimmings. Push the tip of a cocktail stick into the surface to indent the pattern and then set aside to dry.

Cut layers in the cake using a layer cutter

2 Trim the crust from the cake, keeping the rounded top where the cake has risen. Trim around the cake to round off, trimming out four dips with a deeper dip in the centre. Cut two layers in the cake using the layer cutter **(see above)** and sandwich back together using buttercream. Spread a layer over the surface of the cake as a crumb coat to seal the cake and to help the sugarpaste stick.

Tuck excess sugarpaste underneath cake

3 Roll out the lilac sugarpaste and cover the cake completely, pushing gently into the dip at the top taking care not to tear the covering. Smooth down and around the shape, tucking excess sugarpaste underneath **(see above)**. Spread a little buttercream onto the board area where the cake will sit and then place the cake on the cake board. Smooth the surface with a cake smoother and create pleats by rubbing gently in a circular motion with your fingertips.

4 Make the kitten's head first using 210g (7½oz) of white sugarpaste. Roll into a ball and then stick in position at the centre of the cake. Push down gently so the sugarpaste sinks a little and press at the front of the face to flatten slightly. Roll 30g (1oz) into a teardrop shape for the body and roll a sausage using 5g (just under ¼oz) for the tail.

5 Split 15g (½oz) of white into four pieces. Roll one piece into a ball and stick in place for the muzzle. Indent the smile by pressing in with the small circle cutter at an upwards

Indent paws with a knife

angle and mark a line at the top using a knife. Roll two pieces into teardrop shapes for the paws and indent twice into the full end of each by pushing in with the back of a knife **(see above)**. Roll the last piece into a long teardrop shape for the mouse.

6 Roll pea-sized amounts of white into teardrop shapes for ears and indent into the centre of each using the end of a paintbrush. Stick a tiny teardrop of pink into the centre and then stick in position on the kitten's head, slightly angled and pushed forward. Using the remaining white, first shape a tiny teardrop for the lock of hair and then knead white with a little pink until marbled and roll into the ball.

7 With pink, shape a tiny teardrop nose for the kitten and a ball nose, two tiny teardrop ears and a long tail for the mouse. For eyes, roll tiny oval shapes of black for the kitten, cutting twice into the top of each to make eyelashes. For the mouse, roll two tiny black eyes or as they are so small, push in with the tip of a cocktail stick to mark them instead. Moisten the tip of each black

stamen with edible glue and then push gently in place three each either side of the kitten's muzzle.

8 To make the bow, put aside a pea-sized amount of pink and then split the remainder in half. Roll each half into a sausage, each tapering either end and then roll them flat. Indent two pleats at the pointed ends and then loop round sticking together using edible glue. For the centre tie, roll the pea-sized amount into a sausage, press flat and indent two pleats using a cocktail stick. Loop round and stick in position between the bow loops **(see right)**.

Mark pleats in the bow using a paintbrush handle

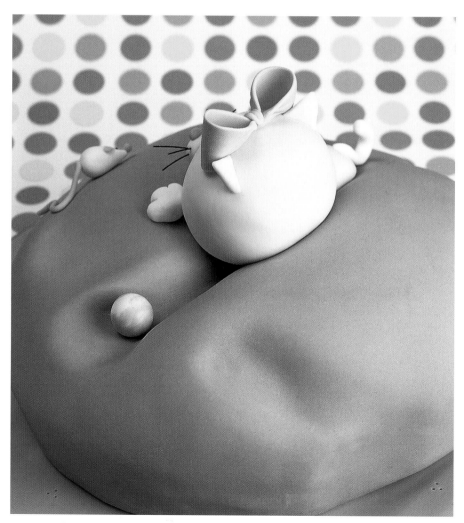

Back view of cake

Travel Bug

Everyone gets the travel bug now and again, some more so than others.
This fun design is especially suitable for a young, carefree gap year
student travelling the world.

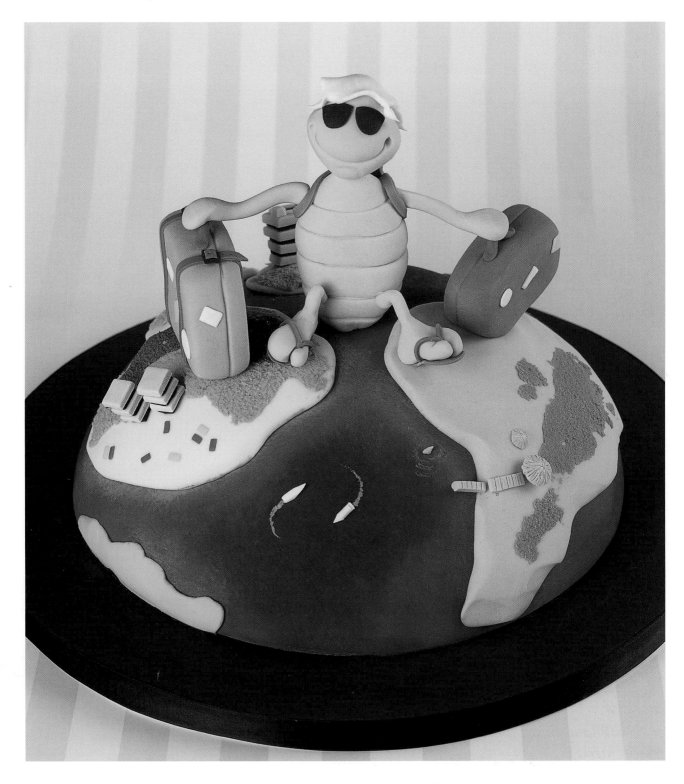

What you will need

See page 7–11 for all recipes and baking chart

- 25cm (10in) round sponge cake
- 35cm (14in) round cake board
- Icing (powdered) sugar in a sugar shaker

Sugarpaste
- 500g (1lb 1¾oz) black
- 600g (1lb 5¼oz) mid blue
- 175g (6oz) cream
- 260g (9oz) dark cream
- 35g (1¼oz) green
- 15g (½oz) dark green
- 15g (½oz) dark golden brown

Modelling paste
- 125g (4½oz) pale brown
- 145g (5oz) dark brown
- 15g (½oz) black
- 150g (5¼oz) lime green
- 10g (¼oz) white
- 30g (1oz) grey
- Pea-sized amount each of red, blue and yellow

- 550g (1lb 3½oz / 2¾c) buttercream
- Edible glue and brush
- White food colouring paste
- Yellow powder colouring

Equipment
- Cake layer cutter
- Large rolling pin
- Small plain bladed knife
- Serrated carving knife
- Cake smoother
- New food-safe scourer (for texture)
- No.6 and no.1 sable paintbrushes
- 3cm (1¼in) and 1cm (¼in) circle cutters
- A few cocktail sticks
- 15–20cm (6–8in) food-safe dowel
- Ruler
- Foam pieces (for support)

Spread the cake surface with buttercream

1 Using a sprinkling of icing sugar to prevent sticking, roll out the black sugarpaste and cover the cake board completely, trimming excess from around the edge. Rub the surface with cake smoother and then set aside to dry.

2 Trim the crust from the cake and slice the top flat. Trim off the top edge to gain a dome shape. Cut two layers in the cake using the layer cutter and sandwich back together with buttercream. Spread a thin layer on the underside of the cake and position centrally on the cake board. Spread buttercream over the surface of the cake as a crumb coat and to help the sugarpaste stick **(see above)**.

3 Roll out the blue sugarpaste and cover the cake completely, smoothing down and around the shape and trimming excess neatly from around the base. Rub the surface with a cake smoother.

4 Using the cream and dark cream sugarpaste, roll out uneven shapes for land and stick in position on the cake using cream on the left side and dark cream on the right. Thinly roll out the green, dark green and dark golden brown sugarpaste and texture by pressing in firmly over each surface with a scourer. Stick in place using both greens for the cream land shapes and the dark golden brown for the darker cream shapes **(see below)**.

Flattened sugarpaste shapes for land

5 Dilute a little of the blue colouring paste with a few drops of water until a watercolour paint consistency. Using the no.6 sable paintbrush, stipple over the blue covering making the colour denser at the centre in between each land shape to depict deeper areas of sea.

6 To make the larger suitcase, shape the pale brown modelling paste into an oblong by pressing gently over the surface with the cake smoother. Indent a line around the sides for the opening using a knife. Repeat for the smaller dark brown suitcase using 90g (3oz).

7 Thinly roll out dark brown modelling paste and cut two strips for the straps on the pale brown suitcase. For the buckle, thinly roll out and cut two tiny black squares and stick a smaller brown square on top of each. Cut further strips for the ends, cutting each to a point and mark holes with a cocktail stick. Roll two sausage shaped handles looping each round and sticking onto the top of each suitcase. Set both suitcases aside to dry.

8 Push the dowel down through the centre of the cake leaving half protruding to help support the bug's body and head. To make the body, roll 90g (3oz) of lime green modelling paste into an oval shape and then pinch both ends until slightly pointed. Mark rings around the body by rolling the back of a knife over the surface. Push down gently over the dowel allowing some of the dowel protrude at the top to help hold the head in place and then secure at the base with a little edible glue.

9 To make the head, roll 35g (1¼oz) of lime green into a ball, pinch slightly angular at the top and bottom and then either side. For the mouth, push the circle cutter inwards and upwards just below halfway, dimpling each corner with the end of a paintbrush. Push gently down onto the dowel and secure with a little edible glue. For the sunglasses, roll a pea-sized amount of black modelling paste into an oval shape, press down to flatten and then cut in half, smoothing gently each cut to round off the top of the glasses. For the kerchief, roll out white modelling paste and cut a small square

measuring 4cm (1½in). Pinch and twist each corner and stick onto the top of his head **(see below)**.

10 To make the legs, first split 15g (½oz) of lime green in half. Roll one into a ball and pinch and roll out a leg at the top, bending halfway. Press down on the rounded end to flatten for the foot and press in at the back either side to shape the heel. Push in gently underneath for the foot arch. Indent the big toe by pressing in with the back of a knife and then pinch up the big toe, rounding it off at the end. Repeat with the second leg.

11 For sandals, split 5g (just under ¼oz) of brown modelling paste in half and roll into sausages, indenting just below halfway. Press down on each to flatten and stick onto the underside of each foot using a little edible glue to secure. Roll two thin sausages of brown and use for the sandal straps. Stick each leg in position using foam pieces for support if necessary.

12 Split the remaining lime green modelling paste and use to make the arms. First roll one piece into a sausage rounding off one end for the hand and press down gently to flatten slightly. Stick in position with the suitcases, again using foam pieces for support if necessary.

13 To make the backpack, using the step picture as a modelling guide, roll 15g (½oz) of brown into a

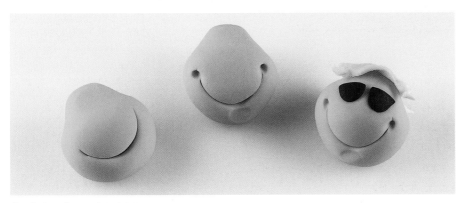

Bug's head step-by-step

43

teardrop shape, marking two parallel lines down the centre using a knife. For the flap, shape a small piece into an oval, press down and stick in position on the top of the backpack. With the remaining brown, cut a strap and buckle as before, using a tiny square of grey modelling paste to make the buckle and cut two long thin straps and loop them around the top of each arm **(see right)**.

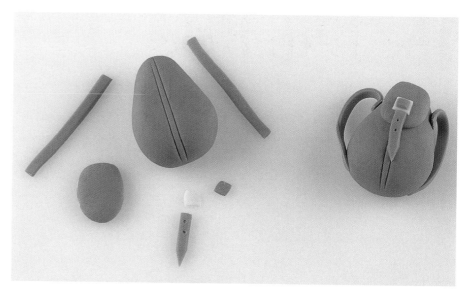

Modelled pieces to complete the backpack

14 To finish, dust the bug's tummy with a little yellow powder colour. Make the three hotels, one large and two small by cutting small grey and slightly smaller black squares and stacking them together with smaller squares at the bottom. For the pool on top of the large hotel, cut tiny strips and stick in an oblong, building it up a little on one side and fill with a few drops of diluted blue food colouring to depict water.

15 Cut tiny oblong shapes for beach towels using red, yellow and blue modelling paste. Cut stickers in white and yellow to decorate the suitcases. Model two tiny white oblong shaped boats, cutting one end of each into a point. Stick a tiny oblong of white onto one boat for a higher deck. For the foam, stipple a little white food colouring at the end of each using a fine paintbrush.

16 Make a pointed fin for the shark and paint faint lines around it with the white paste. With the pale brown modelling paste, make the huts and decking, marking the straw effect roofs and slats using a knife.

Back view of cake

The 19th Hole

The perfect cake for any golfer who thinks there's nothing better than finishing off a good round with a couple of beers. Important time to discuss handicap of course!

What you will need

See page 7–11 for all recipes and baking chart

- 20cm (8in) and 12cm (5in) round sponge cakes
- 25cm (10in) round cake board
- Icing (powdered) sugar in a sugar shaker

Sugarpaste
- 900kg (2lb) green

Modelling paste
- 260g (9oz) golden brown
- 30g (1oz) yellow
- 5g (¼oz) red
- 20g (½oz) lime green
- 45g (1½oz) white

- 450g (1lb / 2c) buttercream
- Edible glue and brush
- Edible gold lustre powder colouring
- Dark brown, green, red and black food colouring
- Confectioners' glaze or a little white vegetable fat

Equipment
- Cake layer cutter
- Large rolling pin
- Small plain bladed knife
- Serrated carving knife
- Cake smoother
- No.1 and no.0 sable paintbrushes
- 25–30cm (10–12in) food-safe plastic dowelling
- 4cm (1½in) circle cutter
- Bone or ball tool
- A few cocktail sticks

1 Trim the crust from each cake and level the tops. Trim the top edge from both cakes to round off. Cut a 5cm (2in) diameter hole in the centre of the small cake. Cut a layer in the larger cake and sandwich back together with buttercream. Spread buttercream on the underside and position slightly off centre on the cake board. Sandwich the smaller cake on top, again slightly off centre for a staggered effect. Spread a layer of buttercream over the surface of the cake to help the sugarpaste stick **(see below)**.

Buttercreamed cake

2 Knead the green sugarpaste until soft and pliable. Roll out and use to cover the cake completely, smoothing down and around the shape and pushing gently into the hole at the top, taking care not to tear the covering. Trim excess from around the edge of the cake board **(see above right)**. Smooth the surface of the cake with a cake smoother.

Trim sugarpaste around base

3 Put aside 5g (just under ¼oz) of golden brown modelling paste and then split the remainder in half. Using the step picture as a guide, model the two beer bottles **(see below)**. To prevent the bottle shapes from sinking and widening at the base, leave each bottle to dry flat. Whilst they are drying, occasionally go back to the bottles and roll each gently backwards and forwards using a cake smoother to prevent the back of each flattening.

Bottle shape

4 Dilute a little dark brown food colouring with a few drops of water until a watercolour paint consistency. Paint streaks over each bottle for a shadow effect. For the bottle tops, split the remaining golden brown in half and roll into ball shapes, pressing each flat. Stick in place on top of each bottle and use the end of the paintbrush to indent around the outside edge of each. Whilst the paste is still moist, rub gold lustre powder over the surface.

5 To make the labels, thinly roll out white modelling paste and cut two circles using the circle cutter. To shape further, cut out small curves from four corners of each, again using the circle cutter. Thinly roll out the white trimmings and cut another circle. Slice across opposite sides of this circle to make two long curved labels for the bottlenecks.

6 Dilute green, red and black food colouring with a few drops of water and paint the labels. Keep the brush quite dry for the green grass effect so it becomes a little streaky. Leave to dry before painting the red banners and flag. With black, paint very fine lines to outline each banner, paint the pole and wording 'Golf' and 'Brew' using the finest paintbrush.

7 Using red, stick a pea-sized ball on the top of the dowelling. Roll thin sausages and shape the numbers one and nine and then set aside to dry. Thinly roll out the yellow modelling paste and cut out a long triangular shape measuring 8cm (3in) in length. Stick in position wrapped around the top of the dowelling. Stick the red numbers in place, curve the end of the flag to give movement and then put aside to dry.

8 To make golf balls, split the remaining white and the lime green modelling paste each in half and roll into ball shapes, indenting over the surface of each using the end of the bone or ball tool. As you press over the surface the ball may become misshapen, so gently roll again and indent carefully until an even dimpled surface is achieved. Stick the golf balls in position on the cake.

9 Push the flagpole down into the cake just beyond the hole at the top, until it reaches the cake board. Stick the bottles in position resting against the pole and supporting each other. To make the bottles shine for a glass effect, paint 3–4 thin coats of confectioners' glaze over the surface allowing each coat to dry in between or rub a little white vegetable fat over the surface taking care not to disturb the painted surface.

For the shine, paint thin coats of glaze over the surface

Sun, Sea and Snorkelling

Paddling happily in crystal clear waters is a very popular pastime. For fun
I've made this poor fellow a tiny bit waterlogged!

48

What you will need

See page 7–11 for all recipes and baking chart

- 20cm (8in) round sponge cake
- 30cm (12in) round cake board
- Icing (powdered) sugar in a sugar shaker

Sugarpaste

1.2kg (2lb 10¼oz) pale blue/green

Modelling paste

- 30g (1oz) flesh
- 25g (just over ¾oz) black
- 5g (¼oz) red
- 10g (¼oz) purple
- 15g (½oz) white
- 60g (2oz) pale grey

- 450g (1lb / 2c) buttercream
- Edible glue and brush
- Pale blue and pale green lustre powder colouring
- Black food colouring

Royal icing

- 30g (1oz) white
- 10g (¼oz) pale yellow

Equipment

- Cake layer cutter
- Large rolling pin
- Small plain bladed knife
- Serrated carving knife
- Cake smoother
- No.6 and no.1 sable paintbrushes
- Two paper piping bags
- Scissors
- No.17 (PME) piping tube (tip) or drinking straw
- A few cocktail sticks

1 Knead 450g (1lb) of the blue/green sugarpaste until soft and pliable. Using a sprinkling of icing sugar to prevent sticking, roll out and cover the cake board completely. Press over the surface with the rolling pin to indent ripples. Trim excess from around the edge and set aside to dry.

2 Trim the crust from the cake and then slice a wedge from the top so it slopes downwards. Use this slice to build up the highest side of the cake to heighten further, allowing it to overlap slightly for waves. Cut two layers in the cake using the layer cutter and sandwich all layers together with buttercream. Spread a thin layer of buttercream over the base of the cake and then place the cake centrally on the cake board. Spread buttercream over the surface of the cake as a crumb coat and to help the sugarpaste stick.

3 Roll out the remaining blue/green sugarpaste and cover the cake completely, smoothing down and around the shape and trimming excess neatly from around the base. To make the waves, unevenly pinch along the edge at the highest side of the cake,

Pinching out the waves

stroking each wave down slightly **(see below left)**. Rub the surface with a cake smoother.

4 Place the white royal icing into a piping bag and cut a small hole in the tip. Dampen the large paint-brush with a little water. Pipe uneven lines along the edge of each wave. As each line is piped, position the damp paintbrush half way into the centre and draw out the royal icing to create faint lines for the sea foam effect.

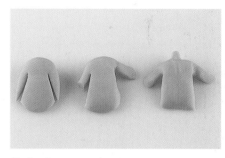

Body shape step-by-step

5 To make the body, slightly flatten a 15g (½oz) ball of flesh modelling paste and cut either side to separate arms, smoothing the ends down level with the work surface. Pinch around the top to make the neck **(see above)**. Mark a line down the centre for the spine and smooth down at the bottom in line with the work surface as before. The body needs to look as though some parts are immersed in water, so when you stick in position on top of the cake, smooth the bottom of the body and ends of each arm level with the cake surface using a little edible glue to secure.

6 For the shorts, press down onto a 10g (¼oz) ball of black modelling paste to flatten slightly and smooth to flatten further around the bottom end, pinching either side to narrow. Make a small cut to separate legs and then stick in position on the body, smoothing around the shape so the base is in line with the surface of the cake.

7 Roll a ball for his head using 10g (¼oz) of flesh and then flatten the face area slightly. Stick in position with head turned to one side. Stick a tiny ball on the centre of his face for his nose and for ears, roll two tiny flesh ball shapes and indent in the centre of each using the end of a paintbrush. Stick in place either side of his head level with his nose. Model two tiny black eyes.

8 Use the remaining flesh modelling paste to make his legs; the immersed one is a ball pressed down flat onto the cake surface and the other a sausage shape pinched gently to narrow the ankle. Use tiny flattened pieces for his forearm and hand. For flippers, split the purple modelling paste in half and roll into teardrop shapes. Press down to flatten each and then roll the paintbrush handle over the surface to indent radiating lines. Stick in position with pea-sized amounts of black for each heel.

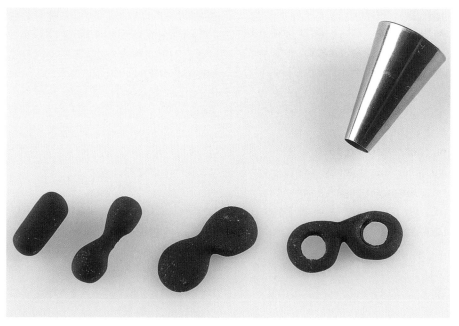

Cut out the lenses with the piping tube

9 Put aside one third of the black modelling paste and use the remainder to make the snorkel and goggles. The mouthpiece is a flattened oval shape and the snorkel a sausage indented into the top end using the paintbrush handle. To make the goggles, roll a small sausage of black modelling paste and roll in the centre to indent and round off opposite ends. Press down to flatten and then cut out the lenses using the piping tube or drinking straw **(see above)**.

10 Pipe the hair using the pale yellow royal icing and the piping bag with a small hole cut in the tip. Use the paintbrush to arrange the hair making it flat against the head around the neck and behind the ears, and then flick up at the front for the spiky look. Thinly roll out and cut a strip for the goggle strap, sticking in place whilst the royal icing is still soft.

11 Thinly roll out the red modelling paste and cut strips to decorate the shorts and around the top of the snorkel. Using blue/green sugarpaste trimmings, make tiny teardrop water splashes for the top of the snorkel and stick tiny sausages into the bottom of the goggles.

12 To make the rock effect around the base of the cake, roll different sized ball shapes of grey modelling paste, pressing down to flatten around the base of the cake. Build up a curved bridge of different sized ball shapes, attaching the end to the side of the cake. Dust around the base of the cake and over the rocks with the pale blue and green lustre powders.

13 Use the white and remaining black modelling paste to make all the fish. There are two types, one a small simple teardrop shape and the other slightly larger, modelled from a flattened circle with a pointed mouth area and top fin, both of which are pinched gently out and the top fin smoothed round gently. To make the fins, cut tiny triangles and indent into each two to three times using a cocktail stick. Stick the fish in position as each is made.

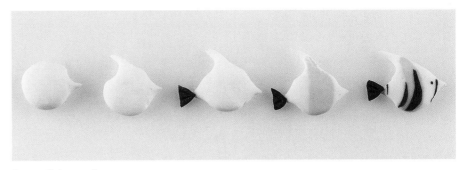

Large fish step-by-step

14 To paint the detailing on the fish, first dilute a little yellow food colouring paste with a few drops of water. Using the fine paintbrush, paint a stripe over the larger fish and stipple a little yellow over the smaller fish. Dilute black as before and paint the black eyes and stripes on both types of fish **(see above)**. Paint tiny lines for eyebrows on the snorkelling figure.

Position fish swimming around rocks

Beach Hut

There are many that'll giggle in recognition at this design of a couple at the seaside, a little rosy from too much sun. It would make a humorous alternative to the usual anniversary cake.

What you will need

See page 7–11 for all recipes and baking chart

- 30cm (12in) square sponge cake
- 30cm (12in) round cake board
- 450g (1lb / 2c) buttercream
- Icing (powdered) sugar in a sugar shaker

Sugarpaste
- 595g (1lb 5oz) white
- 340g (12oz) yellow
- 340g (12oz) blue
- 400g (14oz) cream

Modelling paste
- 100g (3½oz) flesh
- 5g (just under ¼oz) blue
- 20g (¾oz) red
- 60g (2oz) yellow
- 75g (2½oz) white
- Tiny piece of black

- Edible glue and brush
- Pink powder food colouring
- Edible gold lustre powder

Equipment
- Large rolling pin
- Small plain bladed knife
- Cake smoother
- 4cm (1½in) and 2.5cm (1in) circle cutters
- Ruler
- A few cocktail sticks
- New food-safe scourer (for texture)
- Foam pieces (for support)
- No.1, 17 and 18 (PME) plain piping tube (tip)
- No.6 sable paintbrush

1 Trim the crust from the cake and slice the top flat. Cut the cake into four equal squares by cutting in half and then half again. Stack the cakes one on top of the other and to narrow the width, trim 1cm (½in) one side so the cake is slightly oblong in shape. Cut down from the top layer on both sides to shape the pointed roof, taking off the top edge from the second layer of cake.

2 Spread buttercream on the underside of the bottom layer of cake and position on the cake board slightly towards the back. Sandwich all layers together with buttercream then spread a layer over the surface of the cake as a crumb coat to seal the cake and help the sugarpaste stick.

3 Measure the side of the cake up to roof level, reducing the height measurement slightly to allow for the indented lines. Knead 145g (5oz) of white sugarpaste until soft and pliable. Roll out using a sprinkling of icing sugar to prevent sticking and cut a piece to the measurement. Indent lines evenly into the surface using a ruler. Make sure the cut out piece is loose on the work surface and leave to

Indent lines with a ruler

set for a few moments; this will make it easier to position without stretching out of shape. When the sugarpaste has firmed up a little, lift carefully by sliding onto the cake smoother for support and then press in place onto the side of the cake **(see below left)**. Repeat for the opposite side. Following the same method, cut pieces for the back and then the front of the cake using the remaining white.

4 Measure the top of the cake, roll out the yellow sugarpaste and cut a piece for the roof, slightly larger than the measurement. Carefully lift the paste and cover the top of the cake, then press a cake smoother along the edges to straighten them up.

5 Thinly roll out the remaining blue sugarpaste and repeat, covering the roof, cutting slightly larger than before to create an overlap. Thinly roll out the remaining white sugarpaste and cut a square for the doorway. Stick in position on the front of the hut and mark a line down the centre using the ruler. Thinly roll out the remaining blue sugarpaste and cut strips to cover three panels on the front of the hut. Cut strips of yellow modelling paste to edge the door, making the top strip slightly thicker.

6 To cover the board for a sand effect, roll out one quarter of the cream sugarpaste and use to cover the front of the board only. Texture using the scourer pushing in firmly to indent and push up excess against the front of the hut. Cover the sides and then the back using the remaining cream

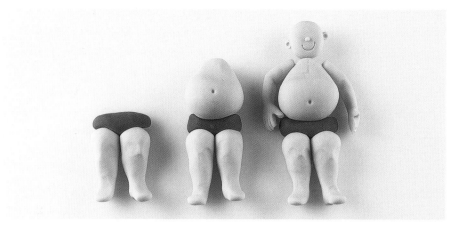

Male figure

sugarpaste, texturing as before and pressing firmly at the joins to remove and blend in. Trim excess from around the cake board edge.

7 To make the lifebuoy, thickly roll out 15g (½oz) of white modelling paste and cut a circle using the large cutter. Cut another circle from the centre making a hoop. Thinly roll out red and cut strips to cover the top and bottom. Stick in place onto the front of the hut supported by the doorframe.

8 Make the legs first using 35g (1¼oz) of flesh modelling paste split into four pieces. To make a leg, roll one piece into a tapering sausage and bend the narrow end round for the foot. Pinch at the back to shape the heel and gently roll the ankle to narrow. Pinch half way and push in at the back to mark the knee. Make three more legs and set aside.

9 For the man's trunks, roll a sausage with the blue modelling paste and press down onto the top of two legs securing with a little edible glue. Leave the legs open slightly for a masculine pose. To make his tummy, roll 30g (1oz) of flesh into a teardrop shape and mark the chest area and belly-button using the paintbrush handle. Stick in position on the trunks and then set aside to dry flat **(see above)**.

10 For the woman's bathing costume, roll 20g (¾oz) of yellow modelling paste into an oval shape for her tummy and stick in place on her legs. Stick the legs together to make a different pose, turning the feet out slightly. Roll an oval shape using 5g (just under ¼oz) of flesh modelling paste and stick onto the top of her tummy. For her chest, split 15g (½oz) of yellow in half, roll into long teardrop shapes and stick in place with the points smoothed up for the costume straps. Set aside flat to dry **(see below)**.

11 Make the arms next using 15g (½oz) of flesh split into four pieces. To make an arm, roll one piece into a sausage rounding off one end for the hand. Press down on the hand to flatten slightly and then make a cut for the thumb, no further than half way and then three shorter cuts across the top to separate fingers. Smooth the surface gently to remove ridges and bend the fingers round. Push the thumb down towards the palm for natural pose. Bend the arm half way as for the knee. Make three more arms.

12 Split the remaining flesh in half and use to make the two heads, noses and ears. The heads are ball shapes and the smiles indented with the no.18 piping tube pushed in at an upwards angle. Dimple the corners of each mouth with a cocktail stick. Model two oval shaped noses.

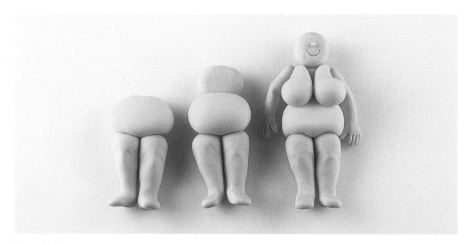

Female figure

For the man's ears, roll two tiny ball shapes and press into each with the end of a paintbrush. Stick in place level with the nose.

13 Thinly roll out black and cut four circles for sunglasses using the no.17 piping tube. To make the kerchief hat, thinly roll out white modelling paste and cut a 2.5cm (1in) square. Pinch at all four corners and then stick in position on top of the man's head. For the sunhat, thinly roll out white and cut a circle using the larger circle cutter. Stick in place encouraging folds and pleats. Roll the remaining white into an oval shape and stick on top. Thinly roll out the remaining yellow and cut a strip for the hatband, crossing it over at the back.

14 To make the beach bag, roll 20g (¾oz) of white into a ball and press down to flatten slightly. Pinch at the top to make a rim for the opening and press either side to narrow slightly. Using a little red, push a small piece into the bag and then thinly roll out and cut circles using the no.17 piping tube and stick in place over the bag for the polka dot pattern. Cut two thin white straps and stick in place looped round and stuck together.

15 Whilst the figures are drying, make the seagull. Using 10g (¼oz) of white modelling paste, roll into an oval shape and pinch gently to indent the neck rounding off the head. Bend the neck round so the head is well balanced and press either side to narrow the head slightly. Pinch at the

Seagull's body shape

end of the body to narrow and then make cuts for tail feathers **(see above)**. For wings, roll teardrop shapes and press each flat. Draw the paintbrush handle over the surface to thin and frill feathers along one side and then stick in place. Model a tiny teardrop of yellow and stick in place for the beak. Stick on tiny black eyes cut from the no.1 plain piping tube.

16 Using edible glue, stick the figures against the door of the hut. Thinly roll out the remaining red modelling paste and cut an oblong for the towel measuring 10 x 5cm (4 x 2in). Texture the surface using the scourer and mark lines using a knife. Fold in half, roll up tightly sticking with edible glue and then stick in place against the man's tummy. If necessary, use foam pieces for support whilst drying.

17 Dust over the sand and around the cake with edible gold lustre powder. Dust a little pink dusting powder over the figures for a rosy, sunkissed look.

Close-up of figures

Sumo Suits

Sumo suits are hilarious and increasingly popular to hire for birthdays, so why not theme the whole party and have a cake in the shape of a fun sumo wrestle. Winner eats all?

What you will need

See page 7–11 for all recipes and baking chart

- 2 x 1L (2 pint) bowl-shaped cakes
- 35cm (14in) round cake board
- Icing (powdered) sugar in a sugar shaker

Sugarpaste
- 500g (1lb 1¾oz) yellow
- 75g (2½oz) green
- 1.2kg (2lb 10¼oz) dark cream
- 160g (5½oz) red
- 160g (5½oz) blue

Modelling paste
- 175g (6oz) dark cream
- 225g (8oz) black
- 30g (1oz) flesh

- 550g (1lb 3½oz / 2¾c) buttercream
- Edible glue and glue brush

Equipment
- Large rolling pin
- Small plain bladed knife
- Serrated carving knife
- Ruler
- Cake smoother
- Foam pieces (for support whilst drying)
- No.17 (PME) piping tube (tip)
- A few cocktail sticks
- 2 lengths of food-safe plastic dowelling

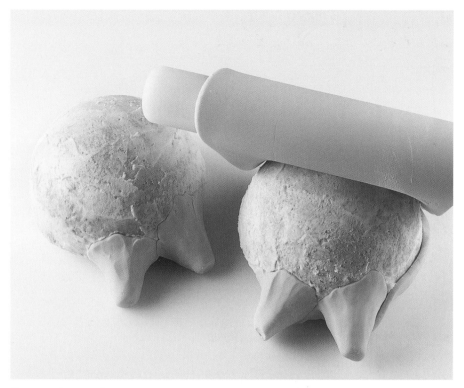

Sugarpaste covering

1 Knead the yellow sugarpaste until soft and pliable. Roll out with a sprinkling of icing sugar to prevent sticking and cover the cake board. Trim excess from around the edge. Thinly roll out the green sugarpaste, cut a 20cm (8in) circle and stick onto the centre of the cake board. Roll gently with the rolling pin to inlay the circle and rub the surface with a cake smoother. Set aside to dry.

2 The top of each cake is the back of a sumo suit with the rounded base as the front. Trim the crust from each cake and level the tops, keeping the rounded edges. Cut two layers in each cake and sandwich back together with buttercream. Place the cakes rounded side up and spread a thin layer over the surface as a crumb coat to seal the cakes and to help the sugarpaste stick. To pad out the legs,

split 160g (5½oz) of dark cream coloured sugarpaste into four pieces and roll into teardrop shapes. Stick the rounded ends against the base of each cake, smoothing the join level with the surface.

3 To cover the back part of the sumo suit, first roll out 175g (6oz) of dark cream coloured sugarpaste. Spread a little buttercream onto the flat side of the cake and then place down onto the rolled out sugarpaste and cut around it. Roll out 360g (12½oz) and use cover the front part of the sumo suit, smoothing around the shape and trimming excess at join **(see above)**. Smooth the join closed with your fingertips. Mark seam lines and the pleats along each using a knife. Indent folds and creases by rubbing gently with your fingers.

Model a hand then stick into the sleeve opening

7 To make the feet, split 10g (¼oz) of flesh in half and roll into sausage shapes. Press down on each to flatten slightly and then make a cut for the big toe, smoothing around the shape to round off and remove ridges. Make three more small cuts for the remaining toes and gently stroke these over **(see below)**. Push into the bottom of each foot to indent the arch and then stick in position on the red sumo suit; because of the cake position, the blue sumo suit doesn't have feet.

4 Cover the second cake in the same way and position both on the cake board using a little edible glue to secure. Push a length of dowelling down through each cake until 5cm (2in) is protruding to help support the head later. Thickly roll out red sugarpaste and cut a strip for the base of a sumo suit, sticking in place wrapped around with the ends tucked underneath. Roll two flattened circles with trimmings for the ankle cuffs. Repeat with blue sugarpaste for the second sumo suit, this time wrapping around the back and tucking excess at the front.

6 For hands, first split 10g (¼oz) of flesh modelling paste into four pieces. To make a hand, shape one piece into a teardrop and press down to flatten slightly. Make a small cut on one side no further than half way for the thumb, and then three more slightly shorter cuts across the top to separate fingers. Gently roll each finger to lengthen and remove ridges, pressing on the tips of each to round off. Pinch at the wrist to narrow and stick into one of the sleeves **(see above)**.

8 Split 200g (7oz) of black modelling paste in half and use to make the two helmets. Roll into rounded teardrop shapes and press into the centre of each by rolling the paintbrush handle backwards and forwards to indent the facial area **(see above right)**. Mark pleats with the handle and smooth to soften them with your fingertip. Push each helmet down onto the dowelling to make a hole, remove and then set aside to dry upright. Split the remaining black in half and model two teardrop shapes for the top of each helmet. Press down on their full end to flatten and then stick in position using a little edible glue.

5 To make the sleeves, split the dark cream modelling paste into four pieces and model into teardrop shapes. Press the full end flat and stick in position on the cake, smoothing the edge in line with the covering. Make a small hole in the sleeve for the hand later by pushing in with the end of a paintbrush.

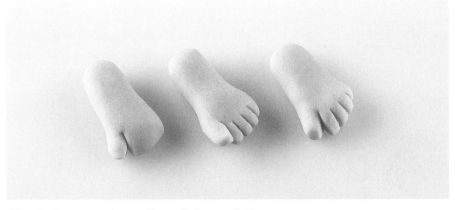

After the toes are cut, smooth gently to round off

9 To make the faces, first set aside a tiny piece of flesh modelling paste for noses and then split the remainder in half. Roll into oval shapes and press down on each to flatten slightly, smoothing down further around the outside edge. Indent the smiles using the large end of the piping tube and dimple each corner with a cocktail stick. Indent laughing eyes using the tip of the piping tube and mark eyebrows using a cocktail stick. Using a little edible glue to secure, assemble each head in position on the cake, each with a tiny oval shaped nose. If necessary, use foam pieces for support whilst drying.

Indent facial area by rolling with a paintbrush handle

Back view

Champagne Bubbles

A newly opened bottle of bubbly spilling those delicious bubbles everywhere makes the perfect cake for any special celebration.

What you will need

See page 7–11 for all recipes and baking chart

- 1 x 10cm (4in) and 2 x 15cm (6in) round sponge cakes
- 25cm (10in) round cake board
- Icing (powdered) sugar in a sugar shaker

Sugarpaste
- 430g (15oz) black
- 945g (2lb 1¼ oz) white

Modelling paste
- 145g (5oz) black

- 550g (1lb 3½oz / 2¾ c) buttercream
- Edible silver and gold food colouring powder
- Edible glue and brush
- 1 tsp white vegetable fat
- 1 tsp clear alcohol (vodka, gin)
- Confectioners' glaze

Equipment
- Large rolling pin
- Small plain bladed knife
- Serrated carving knife
- 20cm (8in) dish
- Length of food-safe plastic dowelling
- Cake smoother
- New plastic scourer
- Template (see page 126)
- No.1 sable paintbrush
- Ruler
- New plastic scourer

1 Using a sprinkling of icing sugar to prevent sticking, roll out 400g (14oz) of black sugarpaste and cover the cake board completely, trimming excess from around the edge. To indent a deep ring, press the top edge of the dish into the centre. Smooth the surface with a cake smoother.

2 Rub a little white vegetable fat over the outside edge of the cake board; this will help the edible silver powder to adhere. Sprinkle the silver powder over the surface, and then rub gently in a circular motion using your fingertips. This will buff the silver and create a good shine. Set aside to dry.

3 Trim the crust from each cake and slice the tops flat. Place one on top of the other with the smaller cake centrally on the top. From this smaller cake, trim the sloping front of the bottle shape and trim around the top edge at the back to narrow. Cut layers in the two larger cakes and then sandwich all layers together with buttercream. Position centrally on the cake board and then spread a layer of buttercream over the surface of the cake as a crumb coat and to help the sugarpaste stick (**see below**).

4 Roll out the remaining black sugarpaste and cover the front of the bottle. Rub the surface with a cake smoother to gain a smooth surface. To help support the top part of the bottle, push the plastic dowelling down through the cake at a slight backwards angle, leaving around 8cm (3in) protruding from the top of the cake.

Spread the surface of the cake with buttercream

Position top of bottle over dowelling

6 For the label, thinly roll out 20g (¾oz) of the remaining black modelling paste and cut out the label shape using the template (see page 126) **(see below)**. With a little edible glue, stick around the neck of the bottle covering up the join. Mix a sprinkling of gold powder with a few drops of clear alcohol and paint the label detailing and fine edging.

7 To gain the shiny glass effect, paint 2 or 3 thin coats of confectioner's glaze over the bottom half of the bottle leaving each coat to dry thoroughly. For the peel around the top of the bottle, shape different sized flattened pieces and glue in place, smoothing the join around the bottom part closed. Smooth some lines down the neck for the foil effect folds.

8 The napkin covering around the bottle is built up in three strips of white sugarpaste to make it more manageable to roll out and prevent tearing when applied. Using 225g (½lb) of white sugarpaste, roll out into a long strip until a thickness

5 To shape the top part of the bottle, roll 125g (4½oz) of black modelling paste into a fat sausage and pinch around the top to narrow the neck of the bottle. Push into the top with your finger to hollow out and pinch up a rim. Press in place on top of the cake, pushing gently down over the dowelling until in line with the bottle covering **(see above).**

Texture the 'bubbles'

of 2–3mm is achieved, the length measuring the circumference of the cake with 10cm (4in) depth. Wrap around the base of the cake encouraging pleats and folds, securing at the front with a little edible glue. Repeat, covering the top part of the napkin, and then the centre strip, using edible glue to secure the joins closed.

9 Thickly roll out the remaining white sugarpaste into a long tapering teardrop shape and texture heavily using the plastic scourer **(see above)**. Stick in position down the front of the cake hiding the napkin joins. Tear pieces away to separate 'bubbles'. If the texture is lost when the bubble effect is applied, texture further with the scourer. To finish, brush the cake with a little edible gold powder, concentrating around the edge of the bubbles to highlight them and into the folds of the napkin.

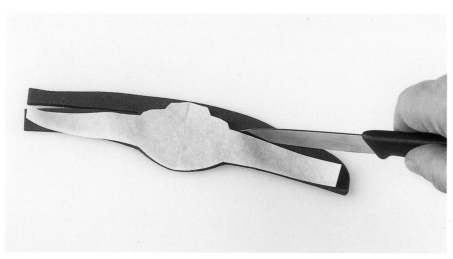

Cut out label using template

Dancing Presents

Suitable for many celebrations by just changing the simple decoration, these animated presents are a sweet and novel idea that are sure to bring gasps of admiration your way.

What you will need

See page 7–11 for all recipes and baking chart

- 15cm (8in) square sponge cake
- 30cm (12in) round cake board
- 400g (14oz / 1¾c) buttercream
- Icing (powdered) sugar in a sugar shaker

Sugarpaste
- 450g (1lb) lime green
- 145g (5oz) orange
- 770g (1lb 11oz) yellow
- 450g (1lb) blue
- 260g (9oz) pink
- 20g (¾oz) pale blue
- 20g (¾oz) pale pink
- 10g (¼oz) white
- 15g (½oz) black

- Edible glue and glue brush

Equipment
- Large rolling pin
- Small plain bladed knife
- Cake smoother
- 3cm (1¼in) and 6cm (2½in) circle cutters
- Ruler
- A few cocktail sticks
- Bone or ball tool
- Foam pieces (for support)

Cut circles from cake board surface

1 Knead the lime green sugarpaste until soft and pliable. Roll out with a sprinkling of icing sugar to prevent sticking and cover the cake board. Trim excess from around the edge. Cut out different sized circles using the cutters and fill with cut out circles of orange sugarpaste **(see below left)**. Rub the surface with a cake smoother. Thinly roll out the remaining orange and cut a strip for the ribbon, sticking in place across the cake board. Set the cake board aside to dry.

2 Trim the crust from the cake and slice the top flat. Cut the cake exactly in half and use one half for the largest present. From the second half, cut a strip 12cm (5in) in length for the medium sized present and use the smaller remaining oblong turned upright for the small present. Shape the sides on all three cakes so each curve slightly, large and small cakes curving right, medium cake curving left. Stand each cake upright and ensure they all sit straight and are level. Trim at the base if necessary. Cover the surface of all cakes with buttercream as a crumb coat to seal and help the sugarpaste stick.

3 Roll out 285g (10oz) of yellow sugarpaste and cut a strip to cover across the top of the large cake and down the sides. Take care when lifting the cut out paste that it doesn't stretch and become misshapen. Smooth over the surface of the covering with the cake smoother **(see above right)**.

Cover cake sides first

4 To cover the back of the cake, moisten around the edge of the side covering with edible glue. Also ensure the buttercream covering is still soft enough to stick to the sugarpaste. If not, add a little more or rework the surface. Roll out 200g (7oz) of yellow and place the back of the cake down onto it and cut around neatly. Repeat for the front of the cake. Spread a little buttercream on the cake board where the cake will sit, leaving room for the remaining two presents and position the cake. Smooth the surface with a cake smoother to remove any imperfections.

5 Roll tiny tapering green sausages and loop round to make spirals for the pattern on the covering. Indent the large smile using the large circle cutter pressed into the surface at an upwards angle. Smooth along the cut to soften and open wider, pushing down at the bottom to create a bottom lip. To dimple the smile, indent into the corners using the bone or ball tool.

6 Cover the medium cake with blue sugarpaste and the small cake with pink sugarpaste as before. To decorate, thinly roll out pale blue sugarpaste and cut circles for the polka dot pattern on the blue present and thinly roll out pale pink and cut stripes for the pink present. Thinly roll out and cut a strip of black for the ribbon on the pink present at least 20cm (8in) in length and stick in position. Cut another strip and then cut into four, looping each round for the bow at the top. Position both cakes on the cake board using a little buttercream at the base.

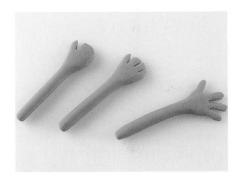

Arms step-by-step

7 To make arms, split 30g (1oz) of yellow in half, 20g (¾oz) for blue and 10g (¼oz) for pink. Roll each into a long sausage rounding off one end. Press the rounded end flat and cut halfway on one side for the thumb. Make two more slightly shorter cuts along the top to separate fingers. Pinch gently to narrow the base of each finger and round off the tips **(see above)**. Moisten the side of the cake with edible glue and leave to become tacky for a few moments before positioning each arm. If necessary, use foam pieces for support while drying.

8 Model pea-sized oval shaped noses and stick on flattened long oval shapes of white for eyes, turning each in at the top slightly to give expression. For pupils, roll six tiny balls using black and press each flat. Stick in place at the bottom of each eye.

9 Make the legs using the remaining sugarpaste. As the pink present is tucked tightly behind the yellow present you only need to make one pink leg. To make a leg, roll the paste into a sausage and bend one third from one end for the foot. Pinch gently at the back for

the heel and push in at the bottom of the foot to indent the arch **(see below)**. Bend the leg half way for the knee and stick in position holding for a few moments until secure. If necessary, use foam pieces for support whilst drying.

Legs step-by-step

Side view

Lucky Numbers

Know of anyone that loves a flutter on the lottery? Tempt fate here and present them with a set of edible lucky numbers. You just never know...

What you will need

See page 7–11 for all recipes and baking chart

- 20cm (8in) square cake
- 30 x 20cm (12 x 8in) oblong cake board
- Icing (powdered) sugar in a sugar shaker

Sugarpaste
- 1.25kg (2lb 12oz) white
- 200g (7oz) black
- 145g (5oz) yellow

- 450g (1lb / 2c) buttercream
- Edible glue and brush

Equipment
- Cake layer cutter
- Large rolling pin
- Small plain bladed knife
- Serrated carving knife
- Cake smoother
- No.4 plain piping tube
- Ball tool

1 Knead 450g (1lb) of white sugarpaste until soft and pliable. Roll out with a sprinkling of icing sugar to prevent sticking and cover the cake board. Rub the surface with a cake smoother and then trim excess from around the edge. Set aside to dry.

2 Trim the crust from the cake and slice the top completely flat. Cut the cake exactly in half and place one on top of the other. Check that they fit together neatly and if necessary trim excess. Sandwich together with buttercream and then spread a layer over the base of the cake. Position the cake on the cake board and spread a thin layer of buttercream over the surface of the cake as a crumb coat to seal the cake and help the sugarpaste stick.

3 Roll out the remaining white sugarpaste and cover the cake completely, smoothing down and around the shape. Because the cake is quite high, the sugarpaste will pleat at the four corners. Stretch each pleat gently outwards and then smooth downwards taking care not to pull and tear at the top. Trim excess from around the base. Smooth the surface with a cake smoother.

4 Using black sugarpaste, roll out and cut two long strips to decorate around the base of the cake, securing the joins closed with a little edible glue. Roll a long tapering sausage and loop round making the question mark sign. Flatten slightly then stick in place with a small dot of black at the bottom.

5 To make the lucky balls **(see below)**, put aside 10g (¼oz) of yellow sugarpaste for the legs later and then split the remainder into six equally sized pieces. Roll into ball shapes and indent a smile into each using the wide end of the piping tube. To dimple each smile, push the end of the paintbrush into the corners. Indent the eye sockets using the small end of a ball tool and roll small balls of white

Lucky ball step-by-step

sugarpaste for eyes. For pupils, thinly roll out black sugarpaste and cut out small circles with the piping tube tip. Stick the lucky balls in a line across the top of the cake. Roll the remaining yellow into a long sausage and cut twelve little legs. Model a flattened oval shaped shoe for the end of each using black.

6 With the remaining black sugarpaste, roll very thin sausages and use to make the different numbers, sticking each in place on top of a lucky ball **(see right)**.

Shape numerals using thin sausages of black sugarpaste

Add numerals to the top of each lucky ball

Playful Puppies

Here's the cutest scene possible, a pile of puppies playfully climbing all over each other. Made from sugarpaste covered cupcakes, simple ideas are often the best.

What you will need

See page 7–11 for all recipes and baking chart

- 12 x sponge cupcakes
- 35cm (14in) round cake board
- 285g (10oz / 1⅛c) buttercream
- Icing (powdered) sugar in a sugar shaker

Sugarpaste
- 500g (1lb 1¾oz) turquoise
- 750g (1lb 10½oz) brown
- 750g (1lb 10½oz) white
- 750g (1lb 10½oz) dark brown
- 15g (½oz) black

- Edible glue and brush

Equipment
- Large rolling pin
- Small plain bladed knife
- Food-safe scourer (for texture)
- Cake smoother
- A few cocktail sticks
- Bone or ball tool
- Foam pieces (for support)

Covering a cupcake

> ### Tip
> These cute puppies look equally sweet presented separately, one for each party guest. If you'd prefer them smaller, simply cut a cupcake in half and use half for the head and the other half for the body.

1 Knead the turquoise sugarpaste until soft and pliable. Roll out with a sprinkling of icing sugar to prevent sticking and cover the cake board. Use the rolling pin to indent the surface for a rippled effect. Trim excess from around the edge. Press the scourer over the surface to texture and then set aside to dry.

2 There are six puppies made with two cupcakes each, one for the body and the other for the head. Two each of the puppies are white, brown and dark brown with different coloured legs, ears, patches and tails. Make puppies one at a time, positioning as each are made. Stick the legs in position last, so the puppies look as though they are playfully climbing over each other.

3 To cover a puppy's body, roll out 115g (4oz) of sugarpaste to 4-5mm thickness. Spread with a layer of buttercream so the sugarpaste will stick and then cover over the top of a cupcake. Gently pick the cupcake up and smooth the covering around and underneath, pressing and smoothing the join closed **(see above)**. Shape one side to narrow the neck area by pinching and smoothing up excess.

4 To cover the puppy's head, cover a cupcake as before and then press the cake smoother onto the facial area to flatten slightly and create a ridge for above the eyes. Push in the small end of the bone or ball tool to open the mouth area and pull gently downwards to create a bottom lip.

5 Use a little edible glue to secure the head to the body. For the muzzle, split 20g (¾oz) of sugarpaste in half and roll into teardrop shapes. Indent whisker holes using a cocktail stick. Split 15g (½oz) in half and roll into teardrop shaped ears, pressing each flat and sticking in position pointing upwards. Bend half way and curve the tips up **(see below)**.

6 For an eye patch, press a small ball down flat and make the edge uneven. Make different sized patches for the body. The eyes are tiny oval shapes of black sugarpaste. Roll an oval shaped black nose. For a tail, roll a tapering sausage using 5g (just under ¼oz) of sugarpaste and stick upright on the body. Take care not to roll the tail too long, otherwise it will flop down. Twist the tip slightly to give movement.

7 To make the back legs, roll 35g (1¼oz) of sugarpaste into a ball and pinch up half for the leg rounding off the foot. Press down on the rounded end to flatten on one side and pinch at the back to narrow the heel.

Stretch out the foot by pulling gently, keeping the toe area rounded and then push into the front with the back of a knife to indent paws.

8 To make the front legs, roll 30g (1oz) of sugarpaste into a sausage rounding off one end. Press the rounded end slightly flat and then push into the front with the back of the knife to indent paws as before.

Shape the covered cupcakes to form the head and body

Princess Cupcakes

The prettiest cherry topped castle any little birthday girl could wish for, complete with ten cute cupcake Princesses, enough for all the little guests to take one home with them.

What you will need

See page 7–11 for all recipes and baking chart

- 10 x cupcakes and 1 x 15cm (6in) round sponge cake
- 35cm (14in) petal-shaped cake board
- 400g (14oz / 1¾c) buttercream
- Icing (powdered) sugar in a sugar shaker
- Edible glue and glue brush

Sugarpaste
- 550g (1lb 3½oz) pale pink
- 370g (13oz) dark pink
- 550g (1lb 3½oz) white

Modelling paste
- 260g (9oz) dark pink
- 45g (1½oz) red
- 45g (1½oz) darkest pink
- 45g (1½oz) mid pink
- 45g (1½oz) pale pink
- 95g (3¼oz) white
- 20g (¾oz) pale flesh
- 20g (¾oz) dark flesh
- 20g (¾oz) pale brown
- 20g (¾oz) mid brown
- 20g (¾oz) dark brown
- Tiny piece of black

Equipment
- Large rolling pin
- Small plain bladed knife
- Cake smoother
- No.18 and no.1 (PME) piping tube (tip)
- Cake layer cutter
- A few cocktail sticks
- White paper cupcake cases
- 10 sugar sticks or lengths of raw, dried spaghetti

1 Knead the pale pink sugarpaste until soft and pliable. Roll out using a sprinkling of icing sugar to prevent sticking and cover the cake board. Trim excess from around the edge and rub the surface with a cake smoother. Set aside to dry.

Tower with window

2 To allow for plenty of drying time, make the tower first. Thickly roll out 115g (4oz) of dark pink modelling paste and cut an oblong measuring 6 x 19cm (2¼ x 7½in). Cut a circle from the centre using the end of a piping tube, then lift and curve round, sticking the join closed with a little edible glue. Set aside to dry **(see above)**.

3 Trim the crust from the cake and slice the top flat. Cut two layers in the cake using the cake layer cutter and sandwich back together with buttercream. Spread buttercream on the underside of the cake and position centrally on the cake board. Roll out the dark pink sugarpaste and cover the cake completely, smoothing down and around the shape and trimming excess from around the base. Smooth the surface with a cake smoother.

4 For the white icing effect edging, split 200g (7oz) of white sugarpaste into three pieces and roll into sausages. Press flat using the cake smoother and then indent along each side to create curls. Leaving room for the doorway at the front, stick in place edging the top of the cake; as these are heavy, only add a small amount of glue to the cake surface and leave for a few moments to become tacky before positioning **(see below)**.

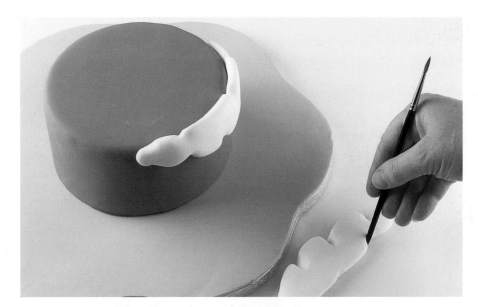

Indent around the icing effect using a paintbrush handle

5 For the door, thinly roll out pale pink modelling paste and cut an oblong 6 x 3cm (2½ x 1¼in). Trim to narrow the sides at the base. Press the paintbrush handle over the surface to indent lines similar to the texture of paper cupcake cases. Stick the door in position with a white icing effect top using 60g (2oz) of white sugarpaste.

6 Using 20g (¾oz) of white sugarpaste, make a step as the white icing effect and smooth down to flatten, pushing up against the front of the door. Stick the tower in position on top of the cake. For the spiral effect roof, roll 160g (5½oz) of white sugarpaste into a 60cm (24in) sausage and loop round on top of the tower securing along the length with edible glue.

7 To hide the join in the large tower, make a small solid tower by rolling a 10g (¼oz) sausage of dark pink, cutting the top and bottom straight. Make an icing top using 10g (¼oz) of white. Make three more towers of different heights and stick in position around base of the cake.

8 To make the cherries, roll different sized balls of red modelling paste and stick in position over the white icing effect. Make a cherry door handle. Use small red ball shapes to decorate the tower window.

9 Spread a little buttercream onto the top of each cupcake. Using the pale pink trimmings, thinly roll out and cut circles to cover the top of

Turn cupcake upside down and add more cake cases for the skirt frills

each and then turn them upside down. Using edible glue, stick four paper cases over the top of each to make the full skirts **(see above)**.

10 There are two Princesses for every colour, darkest pink, dark pink, mid pink, pale pink and white, with their skin colour in pale flesh, dark flesh, pale brown, mid brown and dark brown. To make the skirts, start

with the darkest pink and press down on a 15g (½oz) ball to flatten. Push the paintbrush handle around the sides to indent and frill the edge. Repeat for the second skirt and then split the remainder and roll into two oval shaped bodices. Push a sugar stick down through each body until a little is protruding to help hold the heads in place. Make the dresses in the other colours.

11 To make the arms, take one third of the pale flesh and split into four pieces. Roll into sausages rounding off one end for the hand. Press down on the hand to flatten slightly and then stick in position in the pose, level with the top of the body, each one positioned slightly differently.

Back view

12 Use the remaining pale flesh to make two ball shaped heads and noses. Flatten the facial area slightly. To mark smiles, push the tip of the no.18 piping tube in at an upwards angle and dimple the corners using a cocktail stick. Stick on a tiny ball nose. Repeat making arms and heads with the remaining flesh tones.

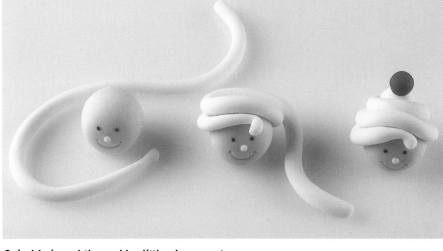

Spiral hair and then add a little cherry on top

Tip
To ensure stability, leave the Princesses to dry or surface set before adding 'hair'.

13 For eyes, thinly roll out the black modelling paste and allow to set for a few moments before cutting all the eyes using the no.1 piping tube. For hair, roll 5g (just under ¼oz) sausages of white, each measuring 20cm (8in) in length with one end rounded off for a curl. Stick in place in a spiral on top of the head, twisting it up at the top. Add a tiny red ball for a cherry bringing it slightly forward to keep the head balanced **(see above right)**. Using a little edible glue, stick the princesses in position around the cake.

Side view

75

Party Hats

A suitable design for any party that can be colour coordinated to the celebration. As Christmas and New Year brings in the season of silly hat wearing, these colours are a stylish alternative for the festive parties.

What you will need

See page 7–11 for all recipes and baking chart

- 3 x 15cm (6in), 2 x 13cm (5in), 1 x 10cm (4in) round cakes
- 35cm (14in) round cake board
- 15cm (6in) and 20cm (8in) round cake cards
- Icing (powdered) sugar in a sugar shaker

Sugarpaste
- 260g (9oz) pale grey
- 260g (9oz) dark red
- 1.6kg (3lb 8½oz) white
- 400g (14oz) dark grey

Modelling paste
- 60g (3oz) dark grey
- 60g (3oz) dark red

- 650g (1lb 7oz / 2¾c) buttercream
- Edible glue and brush
- Food-safe non-toxic silver glitter
- Edible silver lustre powder
- 1–2 tsp white vegetable fat
- 1–2 tsp clear alcohol (vodka, gin)

Equipment
- Cake layer cutter
- Large rolling pin
- Ruler
- No.17 (PME) plain piping tube (tip)
- Medium star cutter
- No.4 sable paintbrush
- Length of food-safe plastic dowelling

Sculpted cake shapes

Please note

Although the glitter is food-safe and non-toxic, it is recommended that excess is brushed away before serving.

1 For the striped effect cake board covering, knead the pale grey and dark red sugarpaste separately until soft and pliable. Roll out using a sprinkling of icing sugar to prevent sticking and cut into 5cm (2in) width strips. Rub a little white fat over the surface of the pale grey strips to give a slight sheen and then rub edible silver powder over the top; the silver will adhere to the white fat giving an even coating. Stick alternate coloured strips over the cake board and then set aside to dry.

2 Trim the crust and level the top of each cake. For the cone shaped hat, first cut a layer in one 15cm (6in) round cake using the cake layer cutter and then use this cake for the case of the hat. Stack on top of this one more 15cm (6in) cake, one 13cm (5in) cake and one 10cm (4in) cake centrally on top of each other. Trim off all top edges and around the shape to obtain smooth, even sides with a point at the top. Sandwich all layers together with buttercream and then spread a layer over the surface as a crumb coat to seal the cake and help the sugarpaste stick. For the dark grey hat, trim the top edge from the remaining 15cm (6in) round cake. Cut layers in the cake using the cake layer cutter and sandwich back together with buttercream. Spread buttercream

on the base of the cake and place centrally onto the 20cm (8in) cake card. Spread buttercream over the surface as before. For the star hat, trim off the top edge from the remaining 13cm (5in) cake to round off making a dome shaped top. Cut a layer and sandwich back together with buttercream **(see below left)**. Spread the base of the cake with buttercream and then place centrally on the 15cm (6in) cake card. Spread a layer of buttercream over the surface as before.

3 Add a little more buttercream to the surface of the cone hat or rework to make it soft to ensure the sugarpaste covering will stick. Roll out 900g (2lb) of white sugarpaste and cut a strip measuring the height of the cake and at least 50cm (20in) in length. Sprinkle with icing sugar to prevent sticking and then roll up. Lift and position against the cone cake, unroll until the covering overlaps and trim away excess at the join and around the base **(see below)**. Use a little edible glue to close the join and rub gently in a circular motion to remove the join completely.

Unroll white covering around cone hat

4 Spread a little buttercream onto the cake board where the cake will sit and then place the cake on the cake board level with the back to leave room for the remaining two cakes. Thinly roll out dark grey modelling paste and cut thick strips to spiral round the cone hat. Cut the strips into no more than 30cm (12in) lengths otherwise they could stretch and become misshapen. Butt the joins together and stick with edible glue, rubbing gently to remove completely. Repeat using dark red modelling paste, cutting thinner strips.

5 To help support the two smaller hats in position, make two lengths of curly 'hair' for the bottom of the cone hat using 175g (6oz) of white sugarpaste for each. Roll into sausages tapering slightly at each end and indent along each side by pushing in with the end of a paintbrush. Stick one either side of the cone hat leaving a 10cm (4in) gap between each at the front.

6 Moisten the edge of the 20cm (8in) cake card with a little edible glue. Roll out the dark grey sugarpaste and cover the cake completely, smoothing down and around the shape and over the cake board, trimming excess from around the edge. Moisten around the base of the hat with edible glue. Thinly roll out the dark grey trimmings and cut a strip for the hatband. Sprinkle with icing sugar to prevent sticking and roll up one end. Position against the base of the hat and unroll around it, trimming excess from the join **(see above)**.

Unroll hatband around base of hat

7 Cover the smaller cake in the same way using the remaining white sugarpaste, cutting a slightly thinner hat band with white sugarpaste trimmings. Thinly roll out pale grey trimmings and cut stars and circles using the star cutter and piping tube, use to decorate the small hat. Dilute a little silver powder with a few drops of clear alcohol until a paint consistency. Paint a thin coat of silver over the hatband for the dark grey hat and over the stars and dots on the white hat. Paint another coat if required.

8 Position the two cakes on the cake board, securing in place with a little edible glue. Sprinkle the dark grey hat with the glitter. Roll out the dark red modelling paste and cut strips of different lengths for the ribbon. As each ribbon is cut, loop around the dowelling to make spirals **(see below)**, leave to set for a few moments and then slide off and stick in place tumbling down from the top of the cone hat.

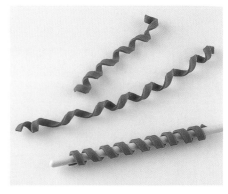

Spiral the ribbon around dowelling

Back view

Musical Notes

This cake is perfect for any music lover, so you're sure to hit the right note when presenting this animated pair.

What you will need

See page 7–11 for all recipes and baking chart

- 34 x 1L (2 pint) bowl-shaped cakes
- 35cm (14in) round cake board
- Icing (powdered) sugar in a sugar shaker

Sugarpaste
- 500g (1lb 1¾oz) white
- 900g (2lb) dark grey

Modelling paste
- 50g (2oz) black
- 125g (4½oz) dark grey

Pastillage
- 85g (2¾oz) dark grey

- 450g (1lb / 2c) buttercream
- Edible glue and brush
- Edible Antique Silver lustre powder
- Red powder food colouring

Equipment
- Cake smoother
- Foam sheet
- Cake layer cutter
- Large rolling pin
- Small plain bladed knife
- Serrated carving knife
- A few cocktail sticks
- Ruler
- Foam pieces

1 Knead the white sugarpaste until soft and pliable. Roll out using a sprinkling of icing sugar to prevent sticking and cover the cake board. Trim excess from around the edge and rub the surface with a cake smoother. Thinly roll out black modelling paste and cut three thin strips each tapering narrower one end. Stick in place curved across the cake board. Set the cake board aside to dry.

2 Make the pastillage frame for the notes next to allow for drying time. Split 60g (2oz) of the pastillage in two and roll into lengths, 20–21cm (8–8¼in), each tapering one end. Roll the remaining pastillage to 17–18cm (6¾–7in) in length, curve round slightly and set all pieces aside to dry flat, preferably on a foam sheet.

Trim crust from all cakes

3 Trim the crust from each cake and level the tops. Sandwich the cakes together with buttercream making two ball shapes. Spread buttercream over the surface as a crumb coat to seal the cakes and help the sugarpaste stick **(see above)**.

4 Roll out 450g (1lb) of dark grey sugarpaste and cover one of the cakes completely, stretching out pleats and smoothing gently downwards **(see below)**. Trim excess from around the base. Smooth the surface with a cake smoother. Repeat for the second cake and position both on the cake board with a small space in between.

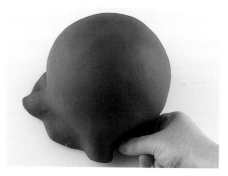

Stretch pleats and smooth downwards

5 To make the horn, roll 45g (1½oz) of dark grey modelling paste into a long teardrop shape and push into the full end to indent, smoothing a neat rim. Whilst the paste is still soft, rub the silver powder over the surface. Model a small flattened ball for the mouthpiece and four tiny ball buttons, rub with silver as before and assemble at the mouth area.

6 For the singing mouth, cut a 6cm (2½in) oval shape out of the covered cake and remove the sugarpaste. Thinly roll out black modelling paste and cut a piece to fill the gap. Roll two thin sausages of dark grey modelling paste and use for the top and bottom lip, smoothing the joins closed with a little edible glue **(see above right)**.

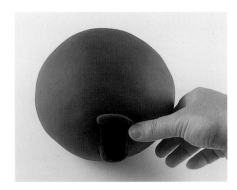

Smooth joins closed

7 Using dark grey modelling paste roll two oval shaped noses and stick in place lengthways. Split 30g (1oz) in half and shape flattened circles for cheeks. Split 5g (just under ¼oz) and roll into long teardrop shapes for the eyelids. Make white eyes for the other face using white sugarpaste trimmings and roll a small sausage for the teeth, press flat and then cut straight at the bottom.

8 Using black modelling paste, make two oval shaped pupils, roll two tiny tapering sausages for eyelashes and four teardrop eyebrows, sticking all in position using a little edible glue. Rub a little red powder colour over the cheeks, lips and noses using your fingertip.

9 For arms, split the remaining dark grey modelling paste into four pieces. To make an arm, roll one piece into a sausage rounding off one end for the hand. Press down on the hand to flatten slightly without indenting. Make a cut half way down on one side for the thumb, with three further slightly shorter cuts across the top to separate fingers. Smooth each finger to lengthen and soften the cuts

(see below). Make all the arms and stick in position, stretching the horn player's arms so they rest on top of the buttons. Use foam pieces for support whilst drying.

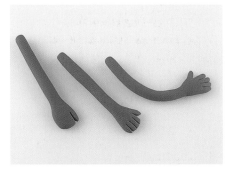

Arm stages step-by-step

10 To stick the frame in position, first stick the two upright lengths in place against the back of each cake. Pad out the space with dark grey trimmings between the frame base and the underside of the cake, smoothing the filling in line with the surface of both the frame and the cake to remove joins. Mix a little dark grey sugarpaste with edible glue until mushy. Using a little of this as a strong glue, stick the bar across the top of the two uprights to complete the frame, again using foam pieces to support whilst drying.

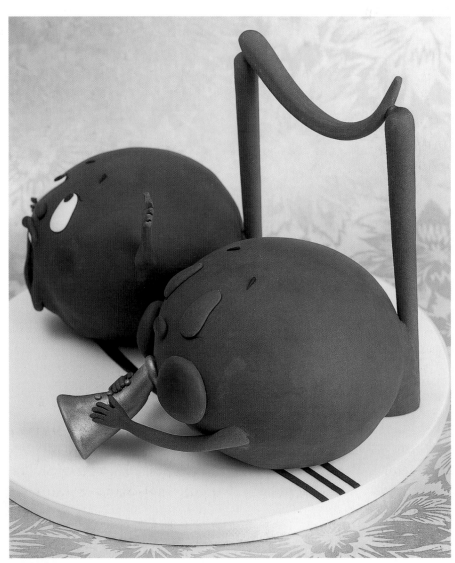

Side view

Fishing Trophy

The perfect cake for any fishermen out there, give your man first prize with this spectacular trophy.

What you will need

See page 7–11 for all recipes and baking chart

- 1 x 23cm (9in) square cake
- 25cm (10in), 20cm (8in) and 15cm (6in) square cake boards
- 10cm (4in) cake card

Sugarpaste
- 900g (2lb) dark grey
- 450g (1lb) white

Modelling paste
- 240g (8½oz) green
- 30g (1oz) dark grey

- 500g (1lb 1¾oz / 2¼c) buttercream
- Edible glue and brush
- Icing (powdered) sugar in sugar shaker
- Edible silver lustre powder
- 1–2 tsp clear alcohol (vodka, gin)

Equipment
- Non-toxic solid glue stick
- Large rolling pin
- Ruler
- Cake layer cutter
- Cake smoother
- 8 lengths of food-safe plastic dowelling
- Pencil
- 6cm (2 ½in) and 5cm (2in) circle cutters
- Bone or ball tool
- No.1 sable paintbrush
- Coordinating cake board ribbon banding

1 Using the glue stick, stick the 20cm (8in) square cake board centrally on top of the 25cm (10in) board and set aside. Trim the crust from the cake and slice the top flat. Cut a 13cm (5in) square from one corner of the cake and then cut two 10cm (4in) squares from the remainder. Using the cake layer cutter, cut a layer in each cake. Sandwich the two smaller cakes together with buttercream. Spread a layer of buttercream over the surface of all cakes as a crumb coat to seal the cakes and help the sugarpaste stick. Spread buttercream onto the underside of the smaller cake and place onto the cake card.

2 Moisten the two large cake boards with a little edible glue. Knead 340g (12oz) of dark grey sugarpaste until soft and pliable. Roll out using a sprinkling of icing sugar to prevent sticking and cover the two cake boards together, smoothing down and around the shape. Trim excess from around the edge and then rub the surface with a cake smoother. Roll out 115g (4oz) and cover the small cake board as before and set all boards aside to dry.

3 Roll out 340g (12oz) of dark grey sugarpaste and cover the large cake, stretching out pleats on the four corners and smoothing down and around the shape. Trim excess from around the base. Smooth the surface with a cake smoother and then lift and position centrally on the large cake board. Roll out trimmings and cut a strip to edge around the base, sticking with a little edible glue.

Use dowelling to support tiers

4 Push four dowelling down through the four corners of the covered cake at least 2cm (¾in) from edge. Mark the top of each using a pencil, taking care not to touch the cake covering. Remove the dowelling and then cut all dowelling to the highest pencil line; this ensures the subsequent tiers sit straight. Push each dowelling back into the cake until level with the surface **(see above)**.

5 Re-work the surface of the 10cm (4in) cake or add a little more buttercream to ensure the sugarpaste will stick to the surface. Roll out white sugarpaste and place one side of the cake down onto it and cut around **(see below)**. Cover the sides first and then the back and front, securing all joins closed with a little edible glue. Use a cake smoother to smooth all sides and

Covering cake sides

then place the cake onto the dark grey covered cake. Dowel the four corners of the cake as before and place the 20cm (6in) cake board on top, securing with a little edible glue.

6 Roll out dark grey sugarpaste and cut a strip to edge around the bottom of the cake. Add another narrower strip on top. Cut out a circle with dark grey modelling paste using the large circle cutter. Cut another circle from the centre using the smaller cutter to make a hoop. Roll out green modelling paste and cut a circle to fill the hoop and then stick in position on the front of the cake. Thinly roll out dark grey modelling paste and cut the numeral using the template (see page 127).

7 Roll 225g (8oz) of the green modelling paste into a teardrop shape and roll the point longer turning it up to curve the back of the fish. Lay the fish flat and cut open the mouth. This will cause the mouth to flatten at the back, so stand upright and smooth to reshape holding the tail so it doesn't sink down. Indent two eye sockets using the small end of a bone or ball tool and smooth around the bottom of each eye by moving the bone or ball tool backwards and forwards **(see above right)**. Lay flat once more until set.

8 For scales, stick tiny teardrop shapes of green over the fish's back. Start at the tail end and overlap each subsequent layer up to the head. Roll thin sausages to edge the top and bottom lip. To make the tail fin, first

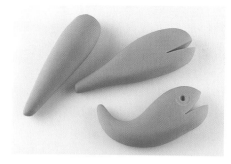

Fish step-by-step

split the remaining green into three pieces. Roll one piece into a teardrop shape and roll flat. Draw a cocktail stick across the surface starting in the centre to thin and frill the edge and repeat, indenting radiating lines from the point **(see below right)**. Stick in position on the tail and smooth the join closed.

9 Make the head fin as before but model a longer teardrop, roll flat and cut the rounded end straight. Use a long side as the base and draw the cocktail stick along it to thin and frill the top. Split the remaining piece in

half and use to make two side fins with three small scales on each. Using white and dark grey trimmings, make the two eyes with two tiny black circles for pupils. Stick the fish onto the top of the cake.

10 Dilute a little edible silver lustre with a few drops of clear alcohol and stipple a little silver colour over the fish's back. Paint the strip edging the base of the centre cake and paint a thin line around the numeral using the paintbrush.

Indent fins with paintbrush handle

Stipple silver colouring down the fish's back

Beer on Tap

Here's a humorous look at life with two drinking buddies a little worse for wear and both too full for even one more drop. They must be in beer heaven.

What you will need

See page 7–11 for all recipes and baking chart

- 3 x 15cm (6in) round cakes
- 15cm (6in) cake card or template
- Icing (powdered) sugar in a sugar shaker

Sugarpaste
- 1.25kg (2lb 12oz) brown

Modelling paste
- 45g (1½oz) pale blue
- 60g (2oz) white
- 90g (3oz) black
- 10g (¼oz) pale brown
- 45g (1½oz) flesh
- 45g (1½oz) dark blue
- 60g (2oz) red

Royal icing
- 45g (1½oz) white
- 20g (¾oz) grey

- 450g (1lb / 2c) buttercream
- Edible glue and brush
- Confectioner's glaze
- Red powdered food colouring

Equipment
- Large rolling pin
- Ruler
- Cake smoother
- 15cm (6in) round cake card or template
- No.1 plain piping tube
- 2 x parchment paper piping bags
- Scissors
- No.6 sable paintbrush

Sandwich cakes together with buttercream

1 Knead 500g (1lb 1¾oz) of brown sugarpaste until soft and pliable. Roll out using a sprinkling of icing sugar to prevent sticking and cover the cake board. Press over the surface to create dimples. Trim excess from around the edge and then set aside to dry.

2 Trim the crust from each cake and slice the top flat. To flatten the base of the barrel, put one cake on top of the other and then slice a little from one side. To narrow the front and back of the barrel, trim around the top edge and then turn upside down and repeat at the opposite end. Sandwich all cakes together **(see below left)** and stand the barrel shape upright. Spread the surface with a layer of buttercream as a crumb coat to seal the cake and help the sugarpaste stick.

3 Roll out 500g (1lb 1¾oz) of brown sugarpaste and cut an oblong to cover across the top of the cake leaving the two ends uncovered. Smooth down and around the shape and smooth the surface with a cake smoother. Indent even lines across the surface by pressing in with a ruler. Scratch a wood grain effect using a cocktail stick. Position the cake on the centre of the cake board.

4 To cover each end of the cake, roll out the remaining brown and cut two circles using the cake card or template. Mark lines across the surface and scratch a wood grain effect as before **(see above right)**. Lift

Mark woodgrain with knife

and carefully press in place using the cake smoother to prevent dimples. Roll out the trimmings and cut two thin strips to edge the joins, marking wood grain as before. Thinly roll out 75g (2½oz) of black modelling paste and cut two strips for the banding. Stick in position and mark the bolts with the tip of a No.1 piping tube.

5 Make a hole in the front of the cake using the end of a paintbrush and moisten with glue. Roll 5g (just under ¼oz) of brown modelling paste into a sausage and indent into one end to open up using the end of a paintbrush. Leave to set for a few moments and then stick in place supported by a piece of foam. Add a little teardrop shaped drip of brown modelling paste at the end.

6 For a wet effect, paint a thin coat of confectioner's glaze over the cake board, leave to dry then repeat until a high shine is achieved. Put the white royal icing into a piping bag and snip a small hole in the tip. Pipe royal icing around the base of the cake concentrating more at the front and back and stipple using the no.6 paintbrush. Repeat around the cake board edge.

7 To make the trousers, roll the pale blue modelling paste into a sausage tapering slightly at one end. Make a cut to separate legs one quarter from the top and then smooth the cut line to soften at the front and back. Cut the bottom of each trouser leg straight. Repeat with the dark blue modelling paste and stick in position on the cake.

8 To make the shirts, roll 45g (1½oz) of white modelling paste into a rounded teardrop shape and mark down the centre for the shirt join with a knife. Mark pleats using the tip. Press the flat of a knife down at the top to indent the chest area. Mark buttons using the no.1 piping tube. Stick in position against the pale blue trousers. Thinly roll out and cut a tiny square pocket and a strip for the collar. Stick the pocket in position with the top open slightly and the collar wrapped around the top of the shirt. For sleeves, split the remaining white in half and roll into short sausage shapes. Roll the paintbrush handle over the end of each and push up to create pleats and folds. Repeat for the red shirt **(see below)**, sticking both in position supported by a piece of foam.

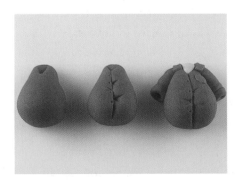

Shirt step-by-step

9 For the belt, thinly roll out the remaining pale brown modelling paste and cut a thin strip to go around the top of the pale blue trousers. Cut a tiny oblong buckle with a smaller oblong on top and then a further tiny strip cut to a point for the end of the belt.

10 Split the remaining black into four pieces and use for the shoes. To make a shoe, roll a sausage and stick onto the end of a trouser leg. Indent the heel by pushing the flat of a knife down just below half way. Make the remaining shoes and stick in position each turned out slightly.

11 To make hands and arms, split 10g (¼oz) of flesh modelling paste into four. Roll one piece into a sausage rounding off one end for the hand. Press the rounded end slightly flatter and then make a cut on one side for the thumb. Make three more slightly shorter cuts across the top to separate fingers and then smooth each gently together and curve round. Push the thumb down towards the palm for a natural pose. Make all the arms.

12 Roll two pea-sized amounts of flesh modelling paste into teardrop shapes, press each flat and then stick point downwards into the top of each shirt. Put aside a pea-sized amount of flesh and then split the remainder in half to make the heads.

Piping hair

13 To make a head, roll into an oval shape and stroke gently downwards to flatten the facial area, pinching at the bottom to narrow the chin. Push the end of a paintbrush into the mouth area and pull downwards to open the mouth. To create cheeks, stroke gently in a circular motion around the cheek area using your fingertip. Roll two small oval shapes for noses. For the closed eyes, press tiny oval shapes flat and cut each in half. Use the straight cut as the base of each eye and stick in position. Mark eyelashes using a cocktail stick.

14 For ears, roll tiny oval shapes and press into each with the end of a paintbrush. Stick in position level with the nose. Pipe the hair using the grey royal icing in a piping bag with a small hole cut in the tip **(see above)**. Pipe the royal icing over each head and use a damp paintbrush to arrange the style, pushing excess down for sideburns. Pipe tiny eyebrows across the top of each eye. Rub a tiny amount of red powder colour over the cheeks, taking care not to add too much.

Water Ride

Often a birthday means a special day out and a trip to a theme park with a few friends is always a good choice. Make the day even more eventful with this birthday treat mirroring some of the joy of the day.

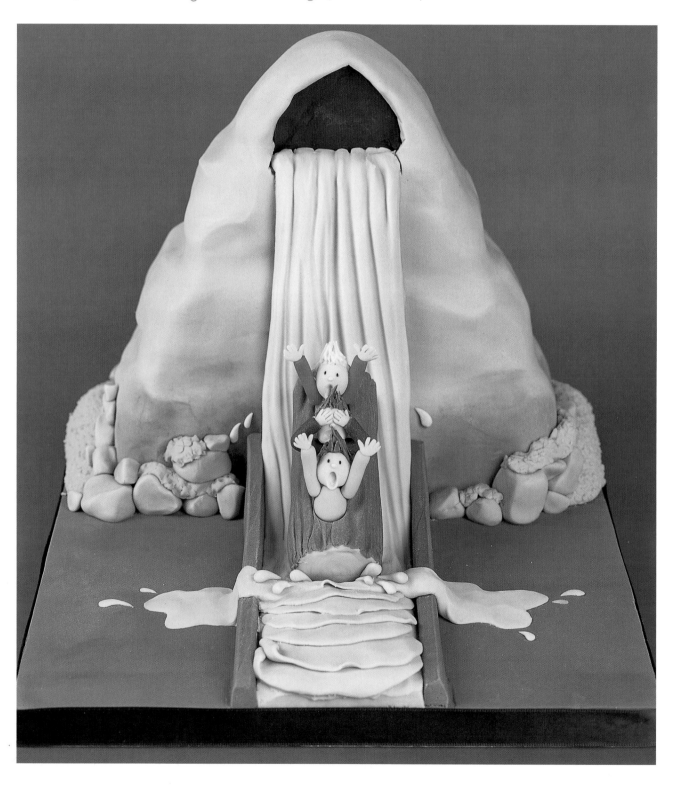

What you will need

See page 7–11 for all recipes and baking chart

- 25cm (10in) square sponge cake
- 25 x 30cm (10 x 12in) oblong shaped cake board
- Icing (powdered) sugar in a sugar shaker

Sugarpaste
- 450g (1lb) purple
- 900g (2lb) pale grey
- 90g (3oz) green
- 145g (5oz) pale blue

Modelling paste
- 20g (¾oz) black
- 115g (4oz) brown
- 15g (½oz) cream
- 5g (just under ¼oz) red
- 5g (just under ¼oz) blue
- 5g (just under ¼oz) green

Royal icing
- 10g (¼oz) brown
- 5g (just under ¼oz) cream

- 500g (1lb 1¾oz / 2¼c) buttercream
- Edible glue and brush
- 3 sugar sticks or lengths of raw, dried spaghetti
- Purple and blue powder food colouring

Equipment
- Large rolling pin
- Small plain bladed knife
- Serrated carving knife
- Ruler
- New scourer (for texture)
- Foam pieces (for support)
- 2 x paper piping bags
- Scissors
- No.6 sable paintbrush

1 Knead the purple sugarpaste until soft and pliable. Roll out using a sprinkling of icing sugar to prevent sticking and use to cover the cake board. Press the rolling pin over the surface to create ripples and then trim excess from around the edge. Set aside to dry.

2 For the two base layers of the water ride, cut an 18cm (7in) strip from the cake and from this piece cut into two oblong shapes measuring 18 x 11cm (7 x 4½in) and 16 x 10cm (6½ x 4in). For the top two layers, cut two pieces from the remaining strip measuring 12 x 6cm (5 x 2½in) and 10 x 5cm (4 x 2in). Stack one on top of the other and then cut a curve in the smallest cake to make the cave **(see below)**. Sandwich all layers together with buttercream and then spread a layer over the surface as a crumb coat and to help the sugarpaste stick.

Shaping the top of the cake

3 Spread the bottom of the cake with buttercream and then position on the cake board towards the back. Roll out the pale grey sugarpaste and cover the cake completely,

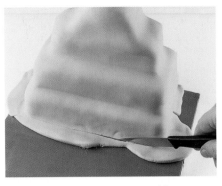

Trimming excess paste around base

stretching out pleats and smoothing down and around the shape. Because of the height, you may find you have a pleat of excess sugarpaste. Pull this up preferably at the back of the cake and pinch closed. Cut excess away and then rub the surface gently to remove the join completely. A little icing sugar on your fingers after smoothing the join will help to make it disappear completely. Trim excess from around base **(see above)**.

4 Smooth around the shape encouraging rock like edges. Cut out the cave at the top, smoothing around the edge to soften slightly. Thinly roll out the black modelling paste and cut a piece to fill this area and reserve trimmings for later.

5 Thickly roll out the purple modelling paste and cut two strips for the cake board edging the water ride, each tapering slightly and measuring no more than 4cm (1½in) at the highest point. Stick in position 8cm (3in) apart.

6 Model different sized angular rock shapes using the remaining grey and build up around the cake securing with a little edible glue. For the grass, thickly roll out green sugarpaste and texture by pressing the scourer over the surface, building this up around the base of the cake and over the rocks.

7 To make the water, roll out the pale blue sugarpaste and cut a strip measuring 6cm (2½in) width. Indent along the surface using the paintbrush handle and stick in position from the cave opening and down the water ride. To make the ripples at the bottom, shape flattened circles with trimmings making the edges fine and stick each overlapping one another. For the overspill and splashes, press blue sugarpaste over the edge of the water ride and onto the surface of the cake board smoothing level with the cake board surface. Roll different sized teardrop shapes for splashes and use to decorate around the cake.

8 To make the log ride, roll the brown modelling paste into a fat sausage shape measuring 10cm (4in) length and cut each end straight. Indent three holes along the top using your fingertip and roll again to reshape. For the ends, split 5g (just under ¼oz) of cream modelling paste in two. Split a pea-sized amount of brown trimmings and knead one each into the cream until streaky and marbled. Roll each into a sausage to straighten the marbling and then roll up into a spiral. Flatten by rolling gently with a rolling pin, keeping the shape circular and use these two circles to cover each end of the log ride.

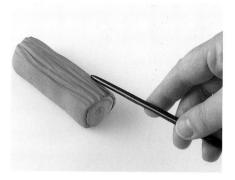

Mark bark effect

9 For the wood bark effect, indent uneven lines over the surface of the log ride by drawing the paintbrush handle along the surface. This will cause the brown to overlap the cream and cover the edges **(see above)**. Turn and repeat for the opposite end and then put aside to dry.

How to build up a figure

10 For the figures **(see above)** use the red, blue and green modelling paste to roll oval shaped bodies and stick in position leaning as far back as possible. Push a sugar stick down into the body of each leaving a little protruding ready to support the heads later.

11 Set aside a small ball of cream modelling paste for later and then split the remainder and roll into

three oval shapes for the heads. Press the facial area a little flat and then push the end of a paintbrush into the mouth area to open up. Stick tiny ball shaped noses onto the centre of each face with tiny black eyes. For ears, model tiny cream oval shapes and press into the centre of each to indent using the end of a paintbrush. Stick in position level with each nose.

12 Model small sausage shaped sleeves each indented in the end using the paintbrush handle to make room for the hands. Stick in position upright secured against the side of each head with the central figure's arms bent halfway towards the eyes.

13 To make the hands, split the remaining cream modelling paste into six pea-sized amounts. To make a hand, roll one piece into a teardrop shape and press slightly flat. Make a cut on one side for the thumb and three shorter cuts along the top to separate fingers. Smooth along each cut to soften and stick in position into the end of each sleeve.

14 Stick the log ride in position on the centre of the water ride. Use a piece of foam sponge to support the centre underneath until dry if necessary. Put the royal icing into piping bags and cut a small hole in the tip. Pipe the hair by squeezing gently upwards into a point. Dust around the base of the cake and over the cake board with the purple and blue powder food colouring using the paintbrush.

Construction Site

It seems these busy builders have a lot to discuss before getting to work. Or perhaps it's an all important tea-break? This fun design is suitable for boys of all ages, including grown-up ones in the construction business.

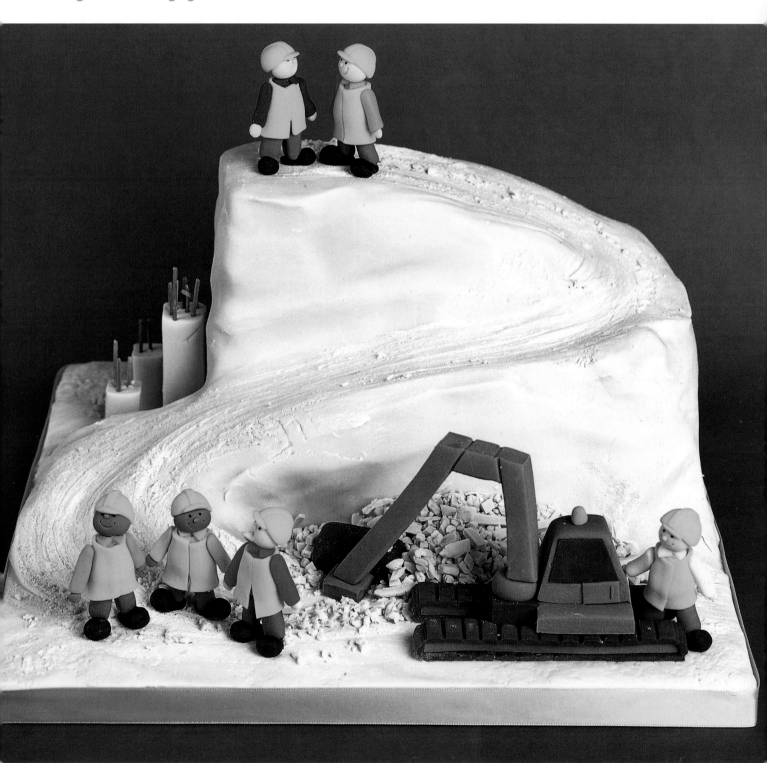

What you will need

See page 7–11 for all recipes and baking chart

- 20cm (8in) square sponge cake
- 30cm (12in) square cake board
- Icing (powdered) sugar in a sugar shaker

Sugarpaste
- 1.25g (2lb 12oz) ivory

Modelling paste
- 75g (2½oz) pale grey
- 35g (1¼oz) dark grey
- 135g (4¾oz) blue
- 60g (2oz) black
- 5g (just under ¼oz) pale blue
- 5g (just under ¼oz) red
- 5g (just under ¼oz) orange
- 5g (just under ¼oz) white
- 45g (1½oz) lime green
- 10g (¼oz) flesh
- 5g (just under ¼oz) pale brown

- 500g (1lb 1¾oz / 2¼c) buttercream
- Edible glue and brush
- White powder colouring
- Edible gold powder colouring

Equipment
- Large and small rolling pins
- Small plain bladed knife
- Serrated carving knife
- New food-safe scourer (for texture)
- No.6 sable paintbrush
- A few cocktail sticks
- No.18 (PME) piping tube or drinking straw
- No.1 (PME) piping tube
- Foam pieces (for support)

Use cake trimmings to extend roadway

1 Trim the crust from the cake and slice the top flat. For a stepped effect, cut a one-third strip from the cake and stack onto the top of the remaining cake towards the back. To create the sloping roadway, trim from the top at the centre, cutting down and out to half of the depth. Trim the opposite end at the next layer in the same way until a sloping roadway is achieved **(see above)**.

2 Spread the underside with buttercream and position the cake on the cake board towards the back. Use the cake trimmings to extend the roadway curving around and down to the cake board surface. Sandwich the layer together with buttercream and then spread a layer over the surface of the cake as a crumb coat to seal the cake and help the sugarpaste stick.

3 Knead the ivory sugarpaste until soft and pliable. Roll out and cover the cake and cake board completely, smoothing down and around the shape and press gently over the cake board surface. Trim excess from around the edge. Press around the sides to indent a rock effect

surface and mark lines along the road using the paintbrush handle creating some tears and crumbs as the surface dries. Texture the cake and cake board further by pressing the scourer over the surface.

4 Roll out the ivory trimmings along with the 30g (1oz) each of pale and dark grey modelling paste and leave to set before cutting repeatedly into the surface to create all the rubble **(see below)**. Moisten the cake board with a little edible glue and sprinkle on the rubble in piles. Brush the surface of the roadway only with a little white powder colour and then brush edible gold over the rubble.

Chop coloured paste to make the rubble

5 To make the concrete blocks, thickly roll out the remaining grey modelling paste and cut strips of different lengths. Push the tip of a cocktail stick into the top of each making holes for the steel. To make the steel, roll dark grey modelling paste into tiny sausages of different lengths and set all pieces aside to dry.

Indenting caterpillar treads

6 For the digger, roll out 15g (½oz) blue modelling paste and cut two strips for inside the caterpillar treads, each measuring 10 x 1cm (4 x ¼in). Thinly roll out 20g (¾oz) of black modelling paste and cut two strips measuring 18 x 0.5cm (7 x ½in). Indent along the length of each using the back of a knife **(see above)** and wrap each around the blue strips trimming excess at join and securing with a little edible glue. Stick in position on the cake board 1cm (½in) apart.

7 For the base of the digger, thickly roll out 10g (¼oz) of blue modelling paste and cut a square measuring 4cm (1½in) and stick in position on top of the wheels slightly off centre. For the cab, model a square of 30g (1oz) blue modelling paste and pinch to narrow the top to create sloping sides. Press the cab down on the work surface to remove any dimples and straighten all sides. Stick in position and then thinly roll out black and cut a window following the shape. Thinly roll out blue trimmings and cut a tiny oblong door panel with a tiny sausage shaped handle.

8 Thickly roll out black modelling paste and cut a 2cm (¾in) square for the base of the digger arm. Stick a small flattened ball of blue onto the top. To make the digger arm, roll a 45g (1½oz) sausage of blue modelling paste and bend round into an arch. Press down onto the surface with a cake smoother to flatten. Cut out the angular shape making the left side slightly longer. Indent join lines at the top using the back of a knife and set aside flat to dry. Roll out blue trimmings and cut a small square for the base of the digger arm and then to make the bucket at the end, roll 15g (½oz) of black modelling paste into a fat sausage and press down to flatten slightly, cutting one side straight.

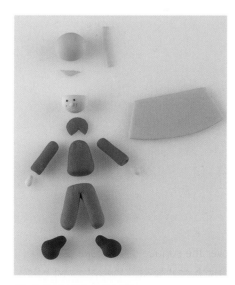

Modelled pieces for figure

9 For the figures **(see above)**, start with the shoes. Split 10g (¼oz) of black modelling paste into twelve equally sized pieces and roll into rounded teardrop shapes. Press onto the top of each to flatten slightly ready for the trousers, but still keep the rounded toe area.

10 To make the trousers, split 30g (1oz) of blue into six pieces. Roll one into a sausage and make a cut three quarters down the length. Smooth down each leg to soften the edges. Cut the end off each trouser leg and cut across the top of the waistband. Stick in position on a pair of shoes, ensuring the figure is standing upright. Repeat for the remaining trousers.

11 To make the top, roll a small rounded teardrop shape, flatten slightly and then cut the bottom straight. Stick in position on top of the trousers and squeeze either side to narrow the body. Make all the remaining tops. Using 20g (¾oz) of lime green, thinly roll out and cut oblong shapes for the tunics, each measuring 4cm (1½in) length and 2.5cm (1in) length. Wrap around each body as soon as they are made, securing at the front. To complete the top, first model a pea-sized amount into a ball and press flat for the collar, and then cut out a small 'v' from the front. Stick in position on top of the body. Roll sausage shaped sleeves, indenting into the end of each with the end of a paintbrush to make a hole ready for the hands later.

12 To make heads, split 10g (¼oz) of flesh into four pieces and 5g (just under ¼oz) of pale brown in half and then roll into ball shapes. Press the facial area slightly flat before indenting either a semi-circular smile using the no.18 piping tube or drinking straw pushed in at an upwards angle or indent an open mouth by pushing in with the end of a paintbrush. Cut off the top of each head sloping the cut slightly towards the back to make a flat surface on which the hat will sit. To make eyes, thinly roll out black and leave to set before cutting all the tiny circles using the no.1 piping tube.

13 To make the hats, split 20g (¾oz) of lime green into six pieces and roll into ball shapes. Cut each in half to make twelve hats and stick in position. Thinly roll out and cut a small strip for the top of each. For the peaks, roll the remainder into a ball and press flat so the edge is fine. Cut twelve strips from around the outside edge of this flattened circle to make all the peaks and stick in position on the front of each hat.

14 Using the remaining flesh and pale brown trimmings, roll tiny teardrop shapes for all the hands and stick in position. Assemble the crane frame using a little edible glue to secure. If necessary, use foam pieces for support whilst drying. Stick the steel into the holes in the concrete blocks and stick in place grouped together. Model an orange light for the top of the cab.

15 Stick the figures in position on the cake using a little edible glue. Position them in little groups turned towards each other and if necessary use foam pieces for support whilst drying.

Close up view of figures

Side view

Queenie Mum

In any family there are always female relatives who deserve to be pampered and spoilt. Complete with the necessities of golden crown, sceptre and cup of tea, this cake will bring a smile to many.

What you will need

See page 7–11 for all recipes and baking chart

- 15cm (6in) round sponge cake and 20cm (8in) square sponge cake
- 30cm (12in) round cake board
- Icing (powdered) sugar in a sugar shaker
- 2 x large rolled sugar sticks

Sugarpaste
- 450g (1lb) pale pink
- 1.25kg (2lb 12oz) pink

Modelling paste
- 225g (8oz) white
- 340g (12oz) pink
- 185g (6½oz) palest pink
- 95g (3¼oz) flesh
- 125g (4½oz) dark pink
- 10g (¼oz) pale lilac
- 10g (¼oz) black

- Edible gold lustre powder
- 450g (1lb / 2c) buttercream
- Edible glue and brush

Equipment
- Templates (see page 126)
- Large rolling pin
- Small plain bladed knife
- Serrated carving knife
- Ruler
- Cake smoother
- Food-safe foam pieces (for support)
- 1cm (¼in) and 2cm (¾in) circle cutters
- No.6 sable paintbrush
- Food-safe scourer (for texture)
- Cake layer cutter

1 Knead the pale pink sugarpaste until soft and pliable. Roll out using a sprinkling of icing (powdered) sugar to prevent sticking and use to cover the cake board. Smooth the surface with a cake smoother and trim excess from around the edge. Make cuts around the edge for a frilled effect, edging with groups of small indentations using the end of a paintbrush. Set the cake board aside to dry.

Bare sculpted cake

2 Trim the crust from each cake and slice the tops flat. Using the template (see page 126) cut out the shape of the back of the throne from the square cake. Stand this piece upright to check that the cake stands completely level and straight **(see above)**. If not, trim and check again. Spread the surface with buttercream to seal the cake and help the sugarpaste stick and set aside.

3 Cut a 4cm (1½in) strip from one side of the round cake and set aside for the footstool later. Cut two layers in the round cake using the cake layer cutter and sandwich back together with buttercream. Spread the surface as before and set aside. To make the footstool, place the small wedge of cake flat side down with the domed surface uppermost. Trim to round off the corners and then spread with buttercream including the underside.

4 To cover the throne seat, roll out 370g (13oz) of pink sugarpaste and cover the round cake completely, smoothing down and around the shape and trimming excess from around the base. Spread the underside with buttercream and position on the cake board towards the back leaving room for the footstool. Smooth the surface with a cake smoother. Push gently in with your fingertip to indent circles and stick a small flattened ball on the centre of each for buttons.

5 To cover the back of the throne **(see below)**, roll out 340g (12oz) of pink sugarpaste and place the back of the throne down onto it and cut

Covering back of throne

around neatly. Make sure the covering is loose on the work surface and then roll out 450g (1lb) and cover over the top, smoothing down and around the shape securing the join closed with a little edible glue. Rub the join in a circular motion to remove the join completely. Smooth the surface, indent and model buttons as before. Moisten the back of the seat with edible glue and then position the seat back against the seat, pressing firmly with the cake smoother to prevent finger marks. Hold for a few moments until secure.

6 To cover the foot stool, first roll 175g (6oz) of the palest pink modelling paste into an oval shape and press flat with the cake smoother, until the same size as the foot stool cake, leaving a depth of around 1.5cm (½in). Roll out the remaining pink sugarpaste and cover the footstool cake completely, smoothing down and around the shape and tucking excess underneath. Position on the foot stool base. Smooth, indent and make buttons as before and then position the foot stool on the cake board against the throne.

7 To make the throne arms, first moisten either side of the throne seat and seat back with edible glue and allow the surface to become tacky. Roll out 160g (5½oz) pink modelling paste and cut two oblong shapes each measuring 8 x 18cm (3 x 7in). Roll up one end of each and stick in position for the chair arms, each supported with a foam piece until dry **(see above right)**. To edge the front of each arm, split 45g (1 1/2oz) of pink

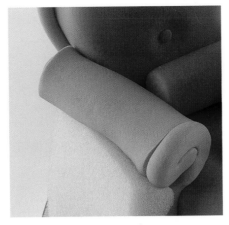

Use foam to support the arms until dry

modelling paste in half and roll each into sausages. Spiral one end of each and stick onto the front of each arm.

8 Split 75g (2½oz) of pink modelling paste in two and roll long sausages each tapering one end to edge the top of the throne back. Stick along the length and then together at the top with a little edible glue. Roll a 10g (¼oz) teardrop and use for the centre, holding for a few moments until secure. Roll the remaining pink modelling paste into a long sausage shaped cushion for the throne back.

9 For the legs, first split 60g (2oz) of flesh modelling paste in half. Roll one into a sausage and bend one end round for the foot. Squeeze gently either side to elongate the foot and push into the bottom to indent the arch. Roll gently to indent the ankle rounding off the foot. Pinch half way to mark the knee, pushing in at the back to shape the leg. Make the second leg.

10 To make the body, roll 90g (3oz) of white modelling paste into a teardrop shape and press down on the full end to flatten slightly. Lay the teardrop shape down and flatten front and back by pressing gently with the cake smoother.

11 To make the cloak, roll out the dark pink modelling paste and cut a piece measuring 12cm (5in) length x 20cm (8in) width. Trim to taper the top slightly and then wrap around the body and legs **(see below)** securing with edible glue and stick in position on the throne. Ensure the body is upright and well balanced. Open up a space for the hand later by smoothing up the edge of the cloak.

Wrap cloak around body

12 To make the head, roll 30g (1oz) of flesh modelling paste into an oval shape and press one side flatter for the face. Indent the smile using the circle cutter pressed in at an upward angle. Make a small hole to mark the nose for later and then using this as a guide, mark a line across the face for the glasses frame curving the line up slightly just above the nose.

13 Indent the glasses as for the smile either side of her nose and just underneath the indented frame line. Push a sugar stick down into the body leaving a little protruding and then stick her head in position with a little edible glue to secure. Stick a tiny oval shaped nose onto the centre of her face hiding the nose indent. Roll two tiny oval shaped black eyes. For the hair, thinly roll out the pale lilac modelling paste and texture by pressing the scourer firmly into the surface. Carefully tear into small pieces and build up around her head until covered completely. Stick on two tiny lilac eyebrows.

14 For the fur effect, roll out white modelling paste into fat sausage shapes to edge around the neck and bottom of the cloak and texture as before. Model a small sausage of white using 10g (¼oz), texture as before and stick in place in a ring around the top of her head. Indent small holes along each fur strip using the end of a paintbrush and stick tiny teardrop shapes of black modelling paste into each.

15 For the crown, thinly roll out 10g (¼oz) of white modelling paste and cut out the crown using the template (see page 126). Loop round, sticking the join together and then stick in position on top of her head. Stick a small ball onto the end of the remaining sugar stick and edge with another crown cut from the sceptre template. Rub the surface with gold powder and push the sceptre down into her lap, securing with edible glue. Support with a piece of foam until dry.

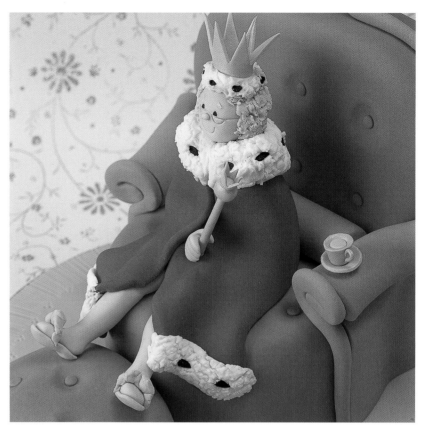

Side view of cake

16 To make the hand, roll the remaining flesh into a teardrop shape and press to flatten slightly. Make a cut on the right side for the thumb, cutting no further than half way. Make three more slightly shorter cuts along the top to separate fingers and smooth to round off. Push the thumb down towards the palm to shape the hand and then stick in position holding the sceptre.

17 Using a little white, make the saucer by first rolling out and cuttng a small circle using the 2cm (¾in) circle cutter. Push this circle gently into a piece of foam to indent. For the cup, roll a small ball into a teardrop shape. Press down on the full end to flatten and then push the paintbrush handle into it to indent a

hole. Pinch around the rim to thin and frill. Press down on the point and then roll across the work surface to straighten the sides. Model a tiny sausage handle and stick in place looped round.

18 Brush gold powder over the surface of the cup and saucer and stick in position on the throne's arm. Put a tiny flattened circle of flesh into the cup for the tea. Use the remaining palest pink modelling paste to make the slippers. To make the soles, roll small sausages and indent into the centre of each, rolling one end slightly smaller for the heel. Press each flat and stick onto the bottom of each foot. Roll two small sausages tapering at either end for the top of each slipper and twist to texture. Stick in position across each foot.

Sleepy Ted

Tucked up sweetly with his little blanket, this enchanting teddy bear will not only be a popular choice for many special celebrations but is also extremely quick and easy to make.

What you will need

See page 7–11 for all recipes and baking chart

- 2L (4 pint) and 1L (2 pint) bowl-shaped sponge cakes
- 1 x 15cm (6in) square sponge cake
- 35cm (14in) round cake board
- Icing (powdered) sugar in a sugar shaker

Sugarpaste
- 800g (1lb 12oz) pale lilac
- 1.14kg (2½lb) golden brown
- 90g (3oz) purple
- 5g (just under ¼oz) black

- 500g (1lb 1¾oz / 2¼c) buttercream
- Edible glue and brush
- Pink powder food colouring

Equipment
- Large rolling pin
- Small plain bladed knife
- Serrated carving knife
- Cake layer cutter
- Cake smoother
- 2 x 13cm (5in) food-safe dowelling
- No.6 sable paintbrush
- Foam pieces (for support)

1 Knead 500g (1lb 1¾oz) of pale lilac sugarpaste until soft and pliable. Roll out using a sprinkling of icing sugar to prevent sticking and cover the cake board. Press the rolling pin over the surface to create ripples and then trim excess from around the edge. Set aside to dry.

2 Trim the crust from all cakes and slice the tops flat where the cakes have risen but leave a rounded edge on the two bowl-shaped cakes. Trim the square pillow cake so it slopes downwards on one side. Cut two layers in each cake using the cake layer cutter and sandwich back together with buttercream. Spread buttercream over the surface of all cakes including the underside as a crumb coat to seal the cakes and help the sugarpaste stick.

3 Roll out the remaining pale lilac sugarpaste and cover the square pillow cake completely, smoothing down and around the shape and trimming excess from around the base **(see below)**. Mark pleats radiating from the centre using the rolling pin then smooth with your hands to soften the indentations. Position the cake on the cake board.

Covering the pillow

4 For the body, roll out 340g (12oz) of golden brown sugarpaste and cover the large bowl cake completely, smoothing down and around the shape and trimming excess from around the base. Position the cake on the cake board up against the pillow. Use a cake smoother to smooth the surface and remove any marks and indentations. Mark the seam line with stitches down the centre using a knife. To cover the head, roll out 225g (8oz) of golden brown sugarpaste and cover as the body and then place onto the pillow. Smooth with a cake smoother and mark a seam line and stitches as before.

Smoothing bottom lip

5 To make the muzzle, roll 125g (4½oz) of golden brown sugarpaste into a rounded teardrop shape and press the cake smoother down onto it to flatten slightly, keeping the round end fuller. Push your finger into the mouth area and stroke up and down rounding the edges and creating an oval shape **(see above)**. Smooth gently at the bottom to indent a ridge to define the bottom lip. Mark a seam line and stitches as before. Stick the muzzle in position using a little edible glue.

6 To make the eyes, roll 2g (¹⁄₂₀oz) of golden brown into an oval shape and press down to flatten. Cut in half and use for the closed eyelids. Split 50g (1¾oz) in half and roll two ball shapes for the ears, indenting into the centre of each with your fingertip, smoothing round in a circular motion to gain a neat edge. Stick the ears in position turned out slightly and supported by the pillow.

7 For the blanket, thinly roll out the purple sugarpaste and cut an oblong measuring 15 x 20cm (6 x 8in). Gather up creating pleats and stick across the teddy's body and draped over the cake board. Press to flatten the blanket where the teddy's hand and arm will be.

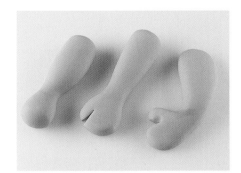

Shaping the arm

8 To make the teddy's arms, split 175g (6oz) of golden brown in half. Roll one into a sausage rounding off one end. Press to flatten slightly and then to indent the thumb, push in on one side using the back of a knife **(see above)**. Smooth around the shape to remove hard edges and then stick in position. Make the second arm indenting the opposite thumb.

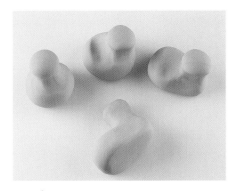

Shaping the foot

9 To help support the legs, push dowels down into the body, leaving 4cm (1½in) protruding. To make a leg, split 225g (8oz) of golden brown in half and roll one into a ball. Pinch up a leg from the top rounding off for the foot. Press down onto the foot to flatten and then press either side to lengthen the foot and narrow the heel **(see above)**. Push the leg down onto the dowelling pressing

against the teddy's body so the top of the leg follows the body's contours. Remove and then set aside to firm up. Repeat for the second leg.

10 To make the nose, roll the black sugarpaste into an oval shape and pinch gently at the bottom to make a softened point and stick in place on top of the muzzle. Brush pink powder colouring onto the cheeks and over the cake board around the cake.

11 When the legs are set, push each onto the dowels and secure at the base with a little edible glue. If necessary, use foam pieces for support whilst drying. Using the golden brown trimmings, model different sized flattened circles for the foot pads and stick in place with a little edible glue.

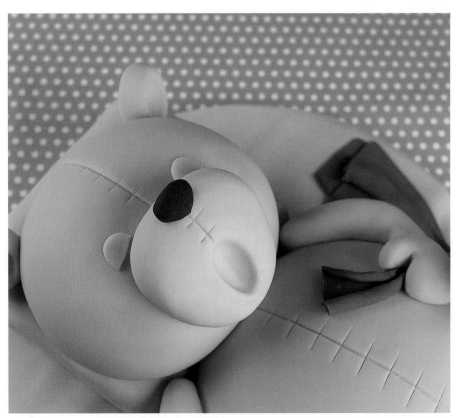

Brush a little pink powder over teddy's cheeks

Baking Day

There are many of us that take on too much and find their kitchen looks as though a hurricane has gone through. So here is a fun scene to bring a smile of recognition to many. At least the results always taste good!

What you will need

See page 7–11 for all recipes and baking chart

- 15cm (8in) square sponge cake
- 30cm (12in) square cake board
- Icing (powdered) sugar in a sugar shaker

Sugarpaste
- 900g (1lb) white
- 260g (9oz) black

Modelling paste
- 145g (5oz) dark cream
- 90g (3oz) red
- 115g (4oz) dark blue
- 65g (2¼oz) flesh
- 115g (4oz) white
- 60g (2oz) pale cream
- Tiny piece of egg yellow
- 115g (4oz) pale brown
- 45g (1½oz) black
- 20g (¾oz) dark brown

- 450g (1lb / 2c) buttercream
- Edible glue and brush
- Edible silver lustre powder
- Sugar stick or length of raw, dried spaghetti
- 1 tsp clear piping gel

Equipment
- Large and small rolling pins
- 5cm (2in) square cutter
- Cake smoother
- Small plain bladed knife
- Serrated carving knife
- Ruler
- New food-safe scourer (for texture)
- A few cocktail sticks
- Bone tool
- No.18 and no.2 (PME) plain piping tubes

1 Knead 260g (9oz) of white sugarpaste until soft and pliable. Roll out using a sprinkling of icing sugar to prevent sticking and cut out 18 squares using the 5cm (2in) square cutter. Repeat using black sugarpaste and stick over the cake board in a chequerboard pattern using a little edible glue to secure. Gently rub the surface with a cake smoother so not to distort the pattern and then set aside to dry.

2 To allow for drying time, make the mixing spoon handle first using 5g (just under ¼oz) of dark cream modelling paste. Roll the paste into a long sausage and set aside to dry.

3 Trim the crust from the cake and slice the top flat. Cut the cake in half and place one on top of the other making an oblong cake. Trim this cake to measure 10 x 18cm

(4 x 7in). Sandwich the layer together with buttercream and then spread a layer over the surface as a crumb coat to seal the cake and help the sugarpaste stick.

4 Roll out 125g (4½oz) of white sugarpaste and place one end of the cake down onto it and cut around. Lift carefully and press the surface with a cake smoother. Repeat with the opposite end and then the back and front, securing the joins closed with edible glue **(see below)**. Rub the surface with a cake smoother. Spread a little buttercream onto the cake board where the cake will sit and then lift and position the cake as quickly as possible to prevent marks. Roll out the remaining white and cut a piece to cover the top of the cake, making it slightly larger than the measurement. Position on top of the cake and press the cake smoother against the cut edges to straighten.

Press sides with a cake smoother

5 Roll out 90g (3oz) of red modelling paste and cut the drawer front measuring 15 x 2.5cm (6 x 1in) and two cupboard doors each measuring 7 x 6cm (2¾ x 2½in). Moisten the area on which the drawer front and doors will be with a little edible glue and then stick in position using the ruler or cake smoother to keep the edges straight. With red trimmings, model four tiny sausage shaped handles and stick in position. Using your fingers, rub the surface of each with a little edible silver powder.

6 To make the figure **(see below)** start with the trousers, roll the dark blue modelling paste into a sausage 12cm (5in) in length tapering slightly fuller one end for the base of the trousers. Make a cut three quarters of the way down to separate the legs and smooth the cut edges to soften. Cut the bottom of each leg straight and reserve trimmings.

7 Split 20g (¾oz) of flesh modelling paste in two and use for the feet. To make a foot, roll one piece into a sausage and indent half way rolling down one side to narrow the heel area.

Press down onto the top to make a flat area for the trouser leg. Repeat for the second foot. For slippers, split 10g (¼oz) of red modelling paste into four pieces and use two for the soles. Roll into sausages and indent into the centre of each by rolling gently down towards the heel to narrow slightly. Press each flat and stick in position on the bottom of each foot.

8 Assemble the figure against the back of the kitchen island. To make the top of each slipper, roll the remaining two pieces into sausages and press the scourer into each to flatten and texture. Stick in position across the top of each foot.

9 To make the girl's top, roll 45g (1½oz) of white modelling paste into a teardrop shape and press to flatten slightly. Press to flatten the neck area and pinch around the bottom to open up so it will fit over the trousers. Mark centrally down the front using a knife.

10 Thinly roll out white modelling paste and cut an oblong for the apron to cover the front of the top and trim so it tapers slightly at the top. Stick in position and then stick in place on the trousers and up against the kitchen island. Thinly roll out white modelling paste and cut a thin strip for the neck strap and another for the apron tie. To make the bow, cut two small strips and stick in position hanging down from the apron tie. Cut two more and loop round for the bow.

Pieces for figure

Cut around bun tin indentations

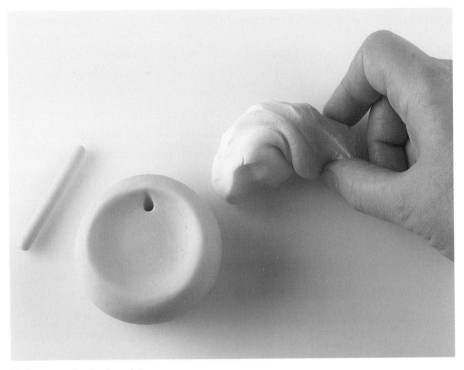

Twist paste for 'cake mix'

11 To make the mixing bowl, roll the remaining dark cream modelling paste into a ball and press down into the centre to indent slightly. Smooth around the edge to neaten the rim. Push a hole into one side using the end of a paintbrush ready to insert the mixing spoon later **(see above)** and then stick the bowl in position with the hole near the edge of the work top and the bowl tipped up slightly.

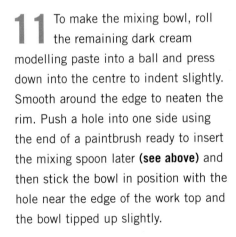

12 To make the flour sack, roll the pale brown modelling paste into a ball and push into the top to make the opening. Pinch out at either end. Texture the sack by pressing the scourer over the surface and stick in position at the side of the kitchen island.

13 To make the large round cake tin, thinly roll out black modelling paste and cut a circle using the 5cm (2in) circle cutter. Cut a strip 2cm (¾in) depth for the cake tin sides, closing the join with a little edible glue. Mark tiny holes at the join with the tip of a cocktail stick. Rub the surface with the silver powder using your fingers and then stick in position.

14 To make the tea towel, thinly roll out 20g (¾oz) of white modelling paste and cut an oblong measuring around 5 x 10cm (2 x 4in). Gather up and stick, draping over the edge of the work top. Thinly roll out red trimmings and cut circles using the large piping tube. Edge the two ends of the tea towel with thinly rolled out strips of black modelling paste.

15 To make the bun tin **(see above)**, thickly roll the remaining black modelling paste and press the small end of a bone tool into the surface in even sections. Cut around the indentations and place the resulting bun tin onto the work top. Reserve the trimmings.

16 For the cake mix, knead the pale cream modelling paste between your fingers pulling outwards and twisting to create texture. Fold some into the mixing bowl, stick some onto the work top, fill one hole of the bun tin and stick some over the floor securing all with a little edible glue.

17 To make the packages, make the box first by cutting a thick oblong shape from 15g (½oz) white modelling paste. Thinly roll out and cut the box flaps and stick in position on top of the box. Stick them upright, leave until set but not dry and then stroke gently to let them drop slightly. Make the bag next using 10g (¼oz) of white modelling paste the same shape as the flour sack. Fill the packages and sack with icing sugar and sprinkle some over the work top and floor.

Side view

18 Roll four oval shaped eggs using flesh modelling paste. Split a pea-sized amount for the cracked egg and push the end of a paintbrush into both, smoothing down the sides to make them hollow with uneven edges. Stick in position on the floor. To make the raw egg, model a tiny flattened circle of egg yellow and spoon a little clear piping gel over it, spreading it out unevenly.

19 To finish the figure, model the right arm supporting the bowl first. Split 20g (¾oz) of flesh modelling paste in half. Roll one half into a sausage and roll gently one end to round off for the hand. Press the hand down to flatten slightly and make a cut for the thumb no further than half way down. Make three more slightly shorter cuts across the top to separate fingers and smooth round to soften the edges. Pinch in half way for the elbow, pinching out at the back to shape the arm. Stick in position using a little edible glue.

20 Stick the spoon handle into the bowl. Make the second arm and stick in position with the hand wrapped around the mixing spoon handle and resting on the edge of the mixing bowl for support.

21 For sleeves, split 5g (just under ¼oz) of white modelling paste in half and roll into ball shapes. Press down on each to flatten and then cut one third from each; the straight edges are the bottom of each sleeve. Stick in position over the top of each arm smoothing around the shape.

22 To make the collar, roll the remaining white into a ball and press down to flatten. Cut a small 'v' from the front and stick in position on top of the body. Insert a sugar stick into the top pushing down until only a little is protruding to help support the head.

23 Thinly roll out blue and red trimmings and leave to set for around 10 minutes before cutting tiny circles using the small piping tube. For ease, let the circles gather in the tube and then pour them out. Pick each up with the glue brush only slightly sticky with glue and then stick in position for the polka dot pattern.

24 To make the head, reserve a little flesh modelling paste for the cheeks and nose and then roll the remainder into a ball. Press down on one side to flatten the facial area and pinch gently either side to shape the chin. Stick in position on the body.

Push the end of a paintbrush into the mouth area and pull gently downwards to open up the mouth.

25 For cheeks, thoroughly knead two tiny ball shapes until as soft as possible and stick onto the cheeks, smoothing in the join with your fingertip. Use a glue brush if there are any stubborn joins and then rub the surface with a little icing sugar on your fingers. Stick on a small ball nose and two tiny black oval-shaped eyes. If you find these tricky to make as they are so small, roll out black and cut two circles with the small piping tube and then roll into oval shapes.

26 For hair, thinly roll out brown modelling paste and cut circles using the large piping tube. Build these up over the head securing with edible glue. Stick a flattened circle of red onto the hair for a hair band and then stick more circles onto this for the pony tail. Brush a tiny amount of red powder colour onto the cheeks.

Back view

Junk Food Mountain

Naughty but nice, nearly everyone likes a little junk food now and again, even if we shouldn't. As this sweet treat would be for a special occasion, you can have a slice of cake guilt free...

What you will need

See page 7–11 for all recipes and baking chart

- 2 x 20cm (8in) round sponge cakes
- 35cm (14in) round cake board
- Icing (powdered) sugar in a sugar shaker

Sugarpaste
- 500g (1lb 1¾oz) cream
- 750g (1lb 10½oz) dark cream
- 145g (5oz) yellow
- 115g 4oz) white

Royal icing
- 60g (2oz) red

Modelling paste
- 120g (4¼oz) pale red/brown
- 500g (1lb 1¾oz) brown
- 500g (1lb 1¾oz) pale cream
- 175g (6oz) red
- 10g (¼oz) blue
- 10g (¼oz) yellow
- 10g (¼oz) green

- Edible glue and brush
- 500g (1lb 1¾oz / 2¼c) buttercream
- Ruler
- Dark brown food colouring paste
- Pale brown powdered food colouring
- Confectioner's glaze
- 1 tsp caster (superfine) or granulated sugar

Equipment
- Large rolling pin
- Small plain bladed knife
- Small palette knife
- Serrated cutting knife
- Cake layer cutter
- No.2 and 3 (PME) plain piping tubes (tip)
- 4cm (1½in) circle cutter
- Cake smoother
- Grater
- Bone or ball tool
- No.6 sable paintbrush
- Dusting brush
- A few cocktail sticks

1 Knead the cream sugarpaste until soft and pliable. Using a sprinkling of icing (powdered) sugar to prevent sticking, roll out and use to cover the cake board. Dimple the surface with your hands and then trim excess from around the edge. Using a palette knife, spread a ring of red royal icing over the surface for the tomato sauce and then set the cake board aside to dry.

2 Trim the crust from each cake and level the tops. Cut an even layer in each cake using the cake layer cutter. Spread buttercream on the underside of one layer and position onto the centre of the cake board for the bun base. For the top of the bun, put the remaining three layers one on top of each other and trim to round off the top **(see below)**. Sandwich the layers together using buttercream and then spread a thin layer over the surface of both cakes as a crumb coat to seal the cake and help the sugarpaste stick.

3 Roll out 315g (11oz) of dark cream sugarpaste and cover the bun base, smoothing down and around the shape and trimming excess from around the base. For the burger meat, roll 315g (11oz) of brown modelling paste into a sausage and use to edge around the top of the bun base making a ring, pinching an uneven surface. Fill this ring with buttercream **(see right)**. Thinly roll out yellow sugarpaste and cut triangles for the cheese. Roll uneven sausages of red, press flat and use for the dripping tomato sauce.

4 Thinly roll out the yellow sugarpaste and cut a strip for the pizza cheese between the bun base and the edge of the tomato sauce. Press this strip firmly in place indenting with your fingertips to achieve an uneven melted cheese effect.

Trim the bun top to round off

Fill burger ring with buttercream

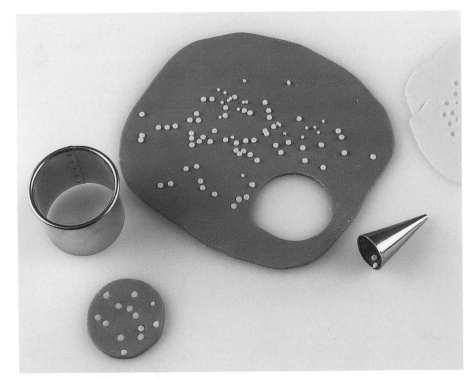

Cutting pepperoni

6 Roll out the remaining dark cream sugarpaste and cover the top of the bun, stretching out pleats and smoothing downwards and around the shape. Cut excess from around the base leaving a 1cm (¼in) strip and tuck this under for a rounded effect. Lift carefully and position on top of the cake and then smooth the surface with a cake smoother.

7 To make the hotdog bun, roll 260g (9oz) of pale cream modelling paste into a fat sausage and press down on the top to flatten slightly. Turn onto its side and slice open two-thirds from the top. Roll the remaining pale red/brown modelling paste into a sausage and stick into the centre of the bun with each end protruding slightly. To make the onions **(see below)**, grate 10g (¼oz) of pale cream modelling paste and stick the grated paste down each side of the hotdog. Roll a thin sausage using 10g (¼oz) of red modelling paste and stick in a wave across the top of the sausage. Stick the hotdog in position across the top of the burger.

5 To make the pepperoni, thinly roll out 45g (1½oz) of pale red/brown modelling paste and sprinkle tiny circles of pale cream modelling paste cut from the piping tubes over the surface. Roll with a rolling pin to inlay until the surface is smooth and even. Cut out circles from the rolled out paste using the circle cutter **(see above)**. Smooth the centre of each to cup slightly and then stick in position around the cake board.

Grate cream paste for onions

8 To make the lolly, first roll out 5g (just under ¼oz) of pale cream modelling paste and cut a strip for the lolly stick measuring 1 x 5cm (¼ x 2in). Cut one end to round off using the circle cutter. Scratch wood grain lines over the surface using a knife. For the lolly, roll the remaining red modelling paste into a fat sausage and press flat with the cake smoother. Cut the bottom straight and push the tip of a knife into the centre at the bottom to make a hole for the lolly stick later. Set both aside to dry.

9 Roll 60g (2oz) of pale cream modelling paste into a long teardrop for the cone. Indent the pattern using the small end of a bone or ball tool and indent lines by pressing in gently with the paintbrush handle. Stick in position resting against the burger bun and the hotdog. For the ice-cream, roll the white sugarpaste into a sausage and press down to flatten slightly with the cake smoother. Wrap around the top of the cone twisting into a spiral and stick the joins closed. Push a hole into the top for the chocolate flake later.

10 To make the chocolate flake, roll 10g (¼oz) of brown modelling paste into a sausage and mark over the surface by cutting lines with a knife. Push a cocktail stick repeatedly into the top, moving around slightly to create curls. Set aside to dry. For the chocolate pieces, thickly roll out the remaining brown modelling paste and indent over the surface using a ruler to mark chocolate blocks. Move the ruler backwards and forwards to widen the indentation and then smooth with your fingertips. Cut around the blocks in sections and stick in position on the cake.

11 To make the chips, thickly roll out the remaining cream modelling paste and cut into strips. Dilute a little brown food colouring paste with a few drops of water to make a translucent wash and paint over each chip. Set aside to dry. Thinly roll out the trimmings and cut circles for the crisps using the circle cutter. Thin and frill the edges of each using the bone or ball tool. For the 'salt', moisten the centre of each with a little edible glue and then sprinkle a little sugar over the surface.

12 Brush the top of the burger bun around the hotdog with a little brown powder colour. Assemble the chocolate flake, chips, lolly with lolly stick and all the crisps in position using a little edible glue to secure. Stick drips of red modelling paste onto the lolly and add some over the pizza. Paint a thin coat of confectioner's glaze over the pizza, tomato sauce and lolly. Paint more layers on the lolly for a high shine effect. Using the remaining brown and the red, blue, yellow and green modelling paste, roll into oval-shaped candies and sprinkle around the cake and cake board.

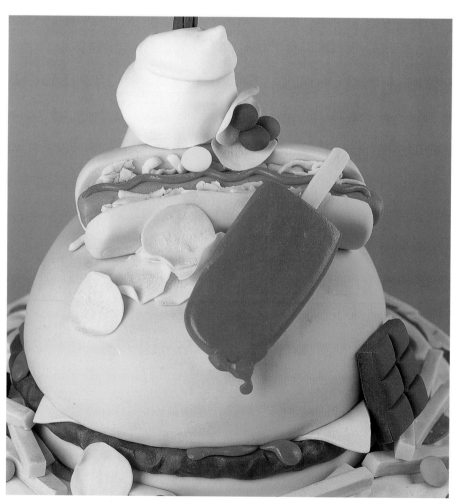

Side view

Castle Ruin

This cake is perfect for anyone who likes to take themselves off for a nice brisk walk with map in hand to see the sights of the local area, so this point of interest is sure to make their celebration complete.

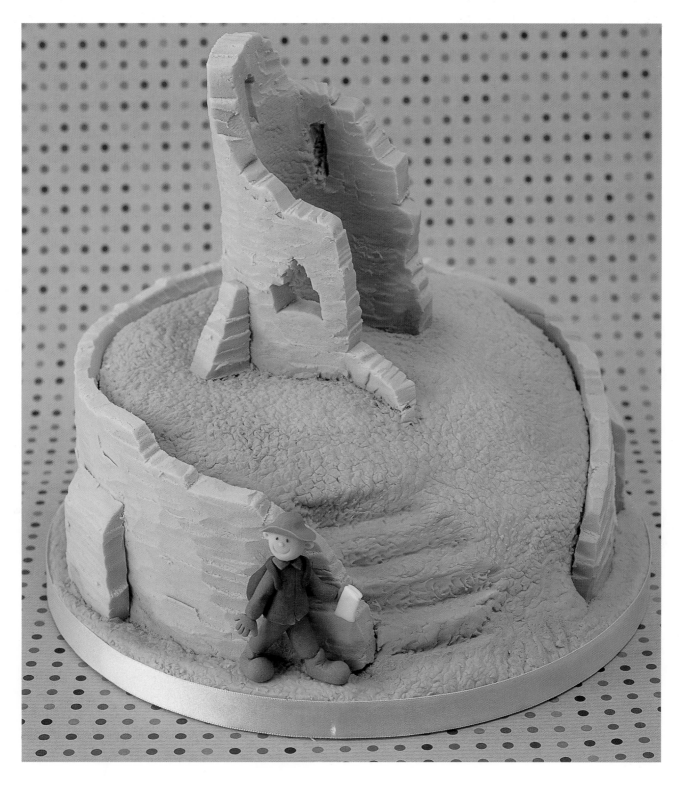

What you will need

See page 7–11 for all recipes and baking chart

- 20cm (8in) round sponge cake
- 25cm (10in) round cake board
- Icing (powdered) sugar in a sugar shaker

Sugarpaste
- 450g (1lb) light green
- 450g (1lb) pale grey

Modelling paste
- 260g (9oz) pale grey
- 10g (¼oz) brown
- 10g (¼oz) blue
- 10g (¼oz) dark green
- 2g (⅟₁₆oz) flesh
- 2g (⅟₁₆oz) white
- Tiny piece of black

- 450g (1lb / 2c) buttercream
- Edible glue and brush
- Green powder food colouring
- Sugar stick or length of raw, dried spaghetti

Equipment
- Large rolling pin
- Small plain bladed knife
- Serrated carving knife
- Ruler
- Template (see page 127)
- Cake layer cutter
- New food-safe scourer (for texture)
- No.6 sable paintbrush
- No.18 and no.1 (PME) plain piping tube

Trim top of cake to slope downwards

1 Trim the crust from the cake keeping the rounded top where the cake has risen. Cut a layer in the cake using the cake layer cutter and sandwich back together with buttercream. Trim one side so the cake slopes down **(see above)** and position these cut pieces on top of the cake to raise it higher and make a slightly uneven but rounded surface. Spread a layer of buttercream onto the base of the cake and position centrally on the cake board. Spread the surface with buttercream as a crumb coat to seal the cake and help the sugarpaste stick.

Texturing grass effect

2 Knead the green sugarpaste until soft and pliable. Roll out using a sprinkling of icing sugar to prevent sticking and cover the top of the cake, down the sloping side and out to the cake board edge on one side

only. Texture the surface with the scourer to create a grass effect **(see below left)**.

3 Trim around the outside edge to neaten ready for the wall positioned against it. Indent the stepped effect on the grass at the front by smoothing the surface with your finger and pinching out the edges, then texture again using the scourer.

4 To make the wall covering the side of the cake, thickly roll out the pale grey sugarpaste and cut a strip measuring 60 x 9cm (24 x 3½in). Lift and use to cover around the sides of the cake with the two ends at the front up against the grass. Cut an uneven top graduating down towards the front of the cake and texture the surface by making small cuts into the surface.

5 Knead all the trimmings together and cut three oblong shapes for the wall supports each measuring 4 x 5cm (1½ x 2in). Stick in position and then cut off the top edge of each so they all graduate towards the wall. Texture the surface as before.

6 To make the castle, thickly roll out the grey modelling paste and cut out the castle shape using the template (see page 127). Stand upright and cut an uneven edge along the top and sides using a knife. Cut out the windows. Texture the stone effect as before, inside and outside. As

Texture walls by slicing off small pieces

you cut you may need to reshape the castle until it sets **(see above)**. With trimmings, make two wall supports and stick in position either side of the castle. Texture the surface as before. When all the texturing is complete, stick the castle onto the top of the cake.

7 Roll out the green trimmings and cut a strip to cover the bare cake board. Texture the surface with the scourer before sticking in position. Disguise the join by texturing further. Dust the cake with a little green powder food colouring concentrating on the base of the castle ruin and wall.

8 To make the walker **(see above right)**, split the brown modelling paste into three pieces, one slightly larger than the others and set this larger piece aside for later. Roll the remaining two pieces into sausages for the boots and pinch up at one end for the top, rounding off the toe area. For trousers, split the blue modelling paste in half and roll one half into a sausage shape. Cut three quarters of the length and smooth to remove ridges. Cut the bottom of each leg straight and stick onto the boots.

Modelled pieces to make the figure

9 For the jacket, roll half of the green into a teardrop shape and press down on the full end to flatten. Press on the point to flatten slightly for the neck area. Mark a line down the centre using a knife and then stick in position on the legs. Using the remaining green, roll a pea-sized amount into a ball, press flat and then cut a small 'v' from one side to make the collar. Split the remainder in half and roll into sausages for sleeves, indenting into the end of each to make a hole for the gloves later.

10 Stick the walker in position against the castle wall. Push a sugar stick down through the top of the body until a little is protruding to help hold the head in place later. Roll out the white modelling paste, cut and fold a small square, to set aside for the map.

11 To make the gloves, roll pea-sized amounts into teardrop shapes and press down to flatten slightly. Make cuts on opposite sides

of each, no further than half way and then make three shorter cuts along the top to separate fingers. Pinch gently at the wrist and stick in position with one hand holding the map.

12 Using the flesh modelling paste, set aside a tiny amount for ears and nose and then roll the remainder into a ball shaped head. Press the front of the face to flatten slightly. Push the no.18 piping tube in at an upwards angle to mark the semi-circular smile. Stick the head in position over the sugar stick and secure at the collar. Roll a tiny oval shaped nose and two ball shapes for ears, indenting into the centre of each using the end of a paintbrush. Stick the nose on the centre of his face with the ears level with the nose.

13 Thinly roll out the black modelling paste and cut two tiny circles using the no.1 piping tube and stick in place for his eyes. To make the hat, roll the remaining brown into a ball and press down around the edge to thin out for the hat rim. Push in at the underside to indent and then stick in position on top of his head, turning it up slightly at the front.

14 For the rucksack, thinly roll out a little blue modelling paste, cut two straps and stick across each shoulder. Roll the rest into a teardrop shape and bend over the point, sticking with edible glue. Stick in position against the walker's back supported by the castle wall.

Techno Freak

This cake was inspired by my eldest son. He's never far from a computer and loves any new technology. I'm sure everybody knows someone who would suit a cake showing all the boxes, wires and remote controls that clutter up our lives!

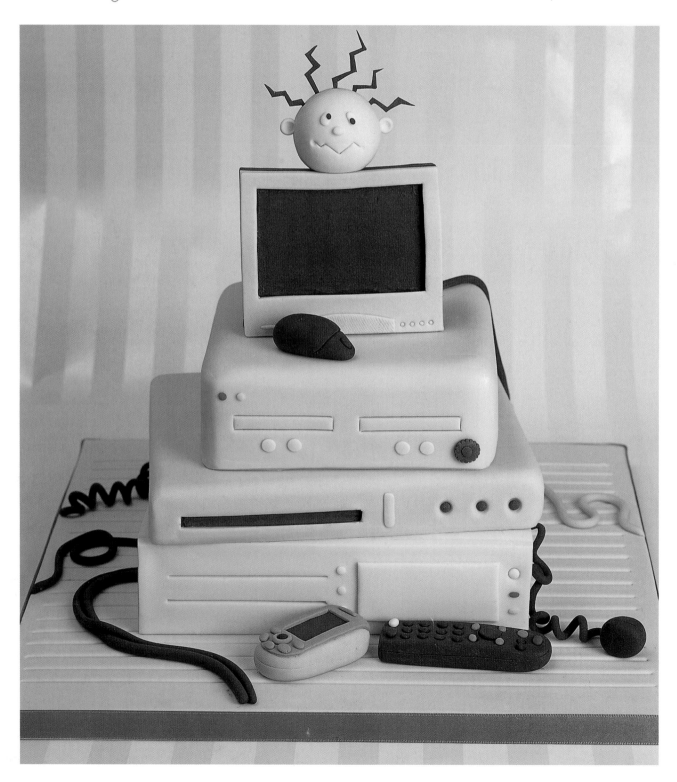

What you will need

See page 7–11 for all recipes and baking chart

- 20cm (8in) and 15cm (6in) square sponge cakes
- 35cm (14in) square cake board
- 20cm (8in) square cake card
- Icing (powdered) sugar in a sugar shaker

Sugarpaste
- 900g (2lb) pale grey
- 700g (1lb 8¾oz) cream
- 370g (13oz) ivory

Modelling paste
- 500g (1lb 1¾oz) black
- 115g (4oz) pale grey
- 10g (¼oz) dark grey
- 75g (2½oz) cream
- Tiny piece each of green, red and white

- 600g (1lb 5¼oz / 2½c) buttercream
- Edible glue and brush

Equipment
- Large rolling pin
- 30cm (12in) ruler or straight edge
- Small plain bladed knife
- Serrated carving knife
- Cake smoother
- Cake layer cutter
- Ball or bone tool
- Length of food-safe dowelling

Cutting zig zag hair

1 Knead 500g (1lb 1¾oz) of pale grey sugarpaste until soft and pliable. Roll out using a sprinkling of icing sugar to prevent sticking and cover the cake board. Smooth the surface with a cake smoother and trim excess from around the edge. Press the ruler over the surface to indent even lines and then set aside to dry.

2 To allow for drying time, make the hair pieces next. Thinly roll out 10g (¼oz) black modelling paste and using the step picture as a guide **(see above)**, cut out five zig zag shaped hair pieces. Set aside to dry.

3 Trim the crust from both cakes and level each top. Cut three even layers in the larger cake using the cake layer cutter and set aside one for the shallow central cake. Sandwich the remaining two layers together for the base cake. Cut a layer in the small square cake and sandwich as before. Spread a layer of buttercream over all three cakes including the bases as a

crumb coat to seal the cakes and to help the sugarpaste stick. Place the single layer cake on the cake card.

Smooth sides with a cake smoother

4 To cover the large base cake, first place it on the cake board. Roll out 90g (3oz) of cream sugarpaste and cut a strip to cover the back of the cake. Repeat covering the two opposite sides **(see above)**. Roll out 340g (12oz) of cream and cover the top, securing the joins closed with edible glue. For the front panel, roll out the remaining cream a little thicker and cut a strip to cover the front. Use a cake smoother over the surface to smooth out any imperfections. Indent two lines into the front panel using a ruler. Indent a hole for the button using the ball or bone tool. Thinly roll out trimmings and cut an oblong door for the front. Model tiny ball shaped buttons and two oval shaped buttons in red and green.

5 Using grey sugarpaste, roll out and cover the single layer cake on the cake card in one piece, smoothing around the shape and trimming excess from the base. Smooth the surface with a cake smoother. Position this cake onto the base cake slightly offset and securing with a little edible glue. Indent three holes for buttons using the bone or ball tool. Cut out a strip at the front and replace with a strip of black cut from modelling paste. Roll three black buttons and model an oblong button using a little pale grey modelling paste.

6 Roll out the ivory sugarpaste and cover the remaining cake completely, smoothing down and around the shape and trimming excess from around the base. Smooth the surface with a cake smoother and then position the cake on top of the central cake. Mark lines for the openings in the front of the cake using a knife and model four flattened ivory buttons with trimmings. Make another red and green button. The large black button is a flattened pea-sized amount of black modelling paste indented with grip lines around the outside using the back of a knife with a smaller flattened ball in the centre.

7 To make the computer screen, thickly roll out 340g (12oz) of black modelling paste until 2cm (¾in) depth and cut two pieces, one for the screen, an oblong measuring 9 x 11cm (3½ x 4½in) and another for the back of the screen measuring 7 x 10cm (2¾ x 4in). Cut a slanted top into the back of the screen by slicing through at an angle. Indent three lines using a knife and push a hole into the base for the lead later. Set both pieces aside to dry.

8 For the screen frame, first moisten around the edge of the screen with a little edible glue. Roll out 60g (2oz) of pale grey modelling paste and place the screen down onto it and cut around. Lift and then cut out the centre measuring 9 x 6cm (3½ x 2½in) **(see below)**.

9 Cut a small oblong shaped panel for the base at the front from thinly rolled out pale grey modelling paste trimmings and cut a curve into the top. Mark a criss-cross pattern over the surface using a knife and stick into position. For buttons, indent four holes using the end of the paintbrush and fill each with a small ball of pale grey. Model a sausage shaped button for the opposite side.

10 Stick the back of the screen into position and then place the screen onto the top of the cake securing with a little edible glue.

11 Using 60g (2oz) of black and 10g (¼oz) of pale grey modelling paste make all the leads. Roll long sausages of modelling paste for the straight leads and spiral some around the dowelling to make

Cut out the screen, removing the paste

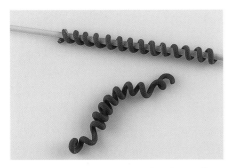

Spiral paste around dowelling for springs

the spring leads **(see above)**. Leave the spring leads to set for a few moments on the dowelling and then gently push off and into position on the cake.

12 To make the plug, roll 5g (just under ¼oz) of black modelling paste into a ball and flatten slightly. Roll the knife around the outside edge to indent a join line. Push the end of a paintbrush into the front three times and fill with tiny sausages of pale grey modelling paste for the pins.

13 To make the remote, roll 45g (1½oz) of black modelling paste into a sausage measuring 10cm (4in) in length and press the cake smoother onto it to flatten. Cut off the top and then indent repeatedly over the surface making holes for the buttons using the small end of a bone or ball tool. Fill the spaces with modelled buttons using white, black, dark grey and red modelling paste.

14 For the mobile, roll the remaining pale grey modelling paste into an oval shape and press down on the top to flatten using a cake smoother. Flatten the top slightly.

Thinly roll out black and cut a piece to cover the front for the screen. To make the screen frame, thinly roll out the dark grey modelling paste and cut a piece to cover the top, curving it round at the bottom. Cut out the screen from the centre. Model oval shaped buttons with a circular button in the centre indented and filled with a black ball. Model a tiny sausage shaped button for the top.

15 Set aside a small piece of cream modelling paste and then roll the remainder into a ball shaped head. Cut a fun zig zag shaped mouth using a knife, dimpling the corners using the end of a paintbrush. For ears, roll two small ball shapes and indent into the centre of each using

the small end of a ball or bone tool and then stick in place half way on either side. Roll an oval shaped nose. Make small holes across the top of the head for the hair pieces later. Roll two tiny oval shaped eyes using white and then model two black pupils. Stick in place 'googly-eyed', one slightly higher than the other . Stick the hair pieces into the holes using a little edible glue and then stick the head in position onto the top of the screen.

16 Using the remaining black modelling paste make the computer mouse. Model a tiny button for the front first then roll the remainder into a teardrop shape. Mark lines using a knife and stick the button in place using a little edible glue.

Back view

White Van Man

The perfect cake for any man who tackles different jobs everyday, or as we all know the pitfalls of moving house, this could be a great alternative welcome to a new home cake.

What you will need

See page 7–11 for all recipes and baking chart

- 25cm (10in) square sponge cake
- 35cm (14in) square cake board
- Icing (powdered) sugar in a sugar shaker

Sugarpaste
- 595g (1lb 5oz) pale blue/grey
- 145g (5oz) black
- 900g (1lb) white
- 340g (12oz) cream
- 75g (2½oz) dark cream
- 90g (3oz) dark turquoise

Modelling paste
- 5g (just under ¼oz) dark cream
- 90g (3oz) white
- 145g (5oz) black
- 60g (2oz) pale red
- Tiny piece of green
- 30g (1oz) pale blue
- 60g (2oz) cream
- 10g (¼oz) flesh

Royal icing
- 10g (¼oz) brown

- 450g (1lb / 2c) buttercream
- Edible glue and brush
- Turquoise and black paste food colouring
- A little cooled, boiled water
- A few drops of clear alcohol (vodka, gin)
- Edible silver lustre powder colouring
- Sugar stick or length of raw, dried spaghetti

Equipment
- Large and small rolling pins
- Small plain bladed knife
- Serrated carving knife
- Ruler
- Cake smoother
- 2.5cm (1in) circle cutter
- No.18 (PME) plain piping tube or miniature circle cutter
- No.4 sable paintbrush
- Template (see page 127)
- Foam sheet and foam pieces (for support)
- Paper piping bag
- Scissors

1 Knead the pale blue/grey sugarpaste until soft and pliable. Roll out using a sprinkling of icing sugar to prevent sticking and cover the cake board. Mark sections using a ruler by indenting different sized squares and oblong shapes. Smooth along each line to distort and round off and then press gently over the surface with your hands to dimple the surface and create a paving stone effect.

2 To allow for drying time, roll 5g (just under ¼oz) of dark cream modelling paste into a sausage for the lamp pole. Using the template, roll out 75g (2½oz) white modelling paste and cut out the two back doors. Indent the windows and detailing and set all pieces aside to dry, preferably on a foam sheet.

3 Trim the crust from the cake and slice the top flat. Cut the cake exactly in half and place one on top of the other. To shape the windscreen, measure 8cm (3in) from one end and cut down at an outward angle to the second layer. Trim both sides of the windscreen so it curves round gently. Trim the bonnet by rounding off the front. Shape opposite sides and the back of the van by slicing down from the top at an outwards angle **(see above right)**.

4 Sandwich the layer together with buttercream and then spread a thin coat over the surface of the cake as a crumb coat to seal the cake and help the sugarpaste stick. Spread the underside with buttercream and then position on the cake board at an angle.

Bare sculpted cake

5 Thinly roll out 90g (3oz) of black sugarpaste and cut a strip measuring 2.5cm (1in) depth to cover around the base of the cake. Sprinkle the surface with icing sugar to prevent sticking and then roll up into a spiral; this will make it easier to lift and position around the base of the cake. Start at the back of the van and unroll the strip around it pressing gently in place with a cake smoother. Smooth the join closed. Thinly roll out the remaining black sugarpaste and cut a piece to cover the back of the van **(see below)**.

Apply thinly rolled out paste to the back

6 Roll out 685g (1lb 8oz) of white sugarpaste and cut a straight edge on the right side. Lift and cover the van completely lining up the straight edge around the back of the van. Smooth around the shape and cut excess away at the bottom, cutting arches to make spaces for the wheels. Using a ruler and a knife, mark the windows, lights and detailing on the van. Push the ruler into the windows to indent them slightly.

7 For wheels, split 90g (3oz) of black modelling paste into four pieces. Roll into ball shapes and press down to flatten slightly using a cake smoother. Indent into the centre of each with the 2.5cm (1in) circle cutter. To mark the detailing, indent the centre of each circle using the no.18 plain piping tube and edge with small holes indented with the end of a paintbrush.

Paint the centre of each wheel silver

8 Dilute a little black food colouring with a few drops of water and paint a very pale almost translucent wash over all the windows. Add a little more colour to darken and paint faint reflection type lines over the surface. Mix the silver powder colouring with the clear alcohol and paint the centre of each wheel **(see above)**, the front lights and a little over each window for a glass effect. Stick each wheel in position using a little edible glue.

9 Set aside a pea-sized amount of black modelling paste and then using the remainder roll out and cut strips for the bumpers, grille, indenting the surface with a ruler and two thin strips for the roof rack. Model tiny door handles, wing mirrors and windscreen wipers. Paint a little silver powder colouring onto the front of each wing mirror.

10 To make the packing boxes, thickly roll out 175g (6oz) of cream sugarpaste and press down onto the top using a cake smoother until around 2.5cm (1in) depth. Cut out a large oblong for the roof rack measuring 10 x 6cm (4 x 2½in). Make another box measuring 6 x 5cm (2½ x 2in) using the remainder and mark the box folds using a knife.

11 For the suitcase, roll the turquoise modelling paste into an oval shape and press down onto the surface using a cake smoother to flatten. Stand the suitcase upright and press down to flatten the bottom. Mark a line around the edge using a knife and stick in position on top of the packing box on the roof rack. Stick tiny pieces of red, white and green modelling paste along the suitcase opening and roll a sausage shaped black handle reserving a minute amount for they man's eyes later. Using the dark cream sugarpaste make two more boxes, marking folds as before.

12 For the mattress, thickly roll out the remaining white sugarpaste and cut an oblong shape

measuring 13 x 9cm (5 x 3½in). Stick in position against the back of the van. Press a cake smoother into the sides of the mattress where the doors will sit, pushing in firmly so the doors will sit straight and positioned almost closed.

13 Dilute a little turquoise food colouring with a few drops of water and paint thin lines in a tartan pattern over the mattress. Dilute the colouring a little more and paint slightly thicker lines next to each. Stick the doors in position and if necessary, use foam pieces to support whilst drying. Roll thin sausages of white modelling paste to edge around the mattress.

14 Push the lamp pole into the cake up against, and supported by, the back of the mattress and secure with a little edible glue. To make the lampshade, roll 30g (1oz) of pale red modelling paste into a teardrop shape and press down on the top and bottom to flatten. Smooth around the top edge to create a dip. Place the lampshade on its side and roll to straighten on the work surface. Push a hole into the centre on the underside so it will fit over the pole. Make cuts around the bottom for the frilled edging using a knife and then stick in position on the pole using a little edible glue to secure. If necessary, use a small piece of foam to support whilst drying.

15 To make the rug, knead 30g (1oz) of cream and the remaining pale red modelling paste together until streaky and marbled. Roll out and cut a circle around 12cm (5in) diameter. Make small cuts all around the edge using a knife to frill and then roll up one end and stick onto the van roof up against the lamp.

16 For the man's shoes, split the 5g (just under ¼oz) of white modelling paste in two and roll into rounded teardrop shapes. Press down onto the centre of each to indent and round off the toe area. To make the trousers, roll the pale blue modelling paste into a sausage and flatten slightly. Make a cut to separate legs one quarter from the top and smooth down each leg front and back to remove the edges. Press on the end of each trouser to flatten and stick the shoes in place. Stand the figure upright up against the back of the van and secure with edible glue.

17 To make his top, roll the remaining cream modelling paste into a ball and press down to flatten slightly using a cake smoother. Make cuts either side for arms and pull both up so they stick outwards. Smooth along the edge of each sleeve to soften and then push into the end of each sleeve with the paintbrush handle to make a hole for the hands later. Pinch down the body to narrow slightly and push in at the bottom with your fingers to indent. Stick in position on the trousers and against the van with edible glue. Push a sugar stick down into the body leaving a little protruding to help hold the head in place.

18 To make the head, first set aside three pea-sized amounts of flesh modelling paste for later and then roll the remainder into an oval shape. Press down to flatten the facial area and then push gently onto the sugar stick securing the base with a little edible glue. Push the end of a paintbrush into the mouth area to open up and move backwards and forwards pulling slightly downwards. Stick a tiny ball nose onto the centre of the face and two tiny oval shaped black eyes. For ears, roll two tiny balls of flesh and indent into the centre of each using a paintbrush.

19 To make the hands, roll two pea-sized amounts of flesh into teardrop shapes and press each slightly flat. Make cuts for the thumbs on opposite sides cutting half way

Hand stages step-by-step

down and then make shorter cuts across the top to separate fingers. Smooth each hand gently to round off and pinch up excess at the wrist area so each hand will slot into the sleeve opening **(see above)**. Stick in position using a little edible glue to secure.

20 For hair, put the brown royal icing into the piping bag and cut a small hole in the tip. Pipe the hair building it up higher at the front. Pipe a tiny amount for sideburns to disguise the ear join.

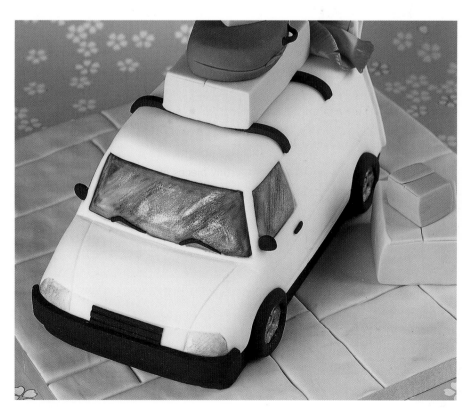
Side view

Prize Allotment

Give this prize specimen to any green fingered gardener or proud allotment holder and you're sure to get a basket of goodies as thanks at the end of the season.

What you will need

See page 7–11 for all recipes and baking chart

- 30cm (12in) square sponge cake
- 35cm (14in) square cake board
- Icing (powdered) sugar in a sugar shaker

Sugarpaste
- 500g (1lb 1¾oz) dark brown
- 900g (2lb) pale brown
- 60g (2oz) pale grey

Pastillage
- 20g (¾oz) pale brown

Modelling paste
- 45g (1½oz) black
- 75g (2½oz) green
- 5g (just under ¼oz) pale green
- 10g (¼oz) brown
- 30g (1oz) dark cream
- 10g (¼oz) red
- Large pea-sided amount of pale blue/grey
- 5g (just under ¼oz) palest brown
- Large pea-sized amount of pale yellow

Royal icing
- 45g (1½oz) green

- 500g (1lb 1¾oz / 2¼c) buttercream
- Edible glue and brush
- Edible Silver and Chestnut brown powder colour
- Clear piping gel

Equipment
- Large rolling pin
- Small plain bladed knife
- Serrated cutting knife
- Ruler
- 2.5cm (1in) square cutter
- Bone or ball tool
- Leaf veiner or dried bay leaf
- A few cocktail sticks
- Scissors
- 2 x paper piping bags
- Small piece of voile net (optional)
- Foam pieces (for support)
- No.6 sable paintbrush

1 Knead the dark brown sugarpaste until soft and pliable. Roll out using a sprinkling of icing sugar to prevent sticking and cover the cake board. Indent the surface by pressing firmly over the surface with your hands and then trim excess from around the edge. With trimmings, build up the areas where the scarecrow and canes will be inserted by sticking excess paste in mounds onto the surface, smoothing the joins closed. Set the cake board aside to dry.

2 To allow for drying time, roll 5g (just under ¼oz) of pastillage into a sausage measuring 8cm (3in) length for the scarecrow pole. Using the remaining pastillage, roll four thin canes for the beans, each measuring 8cm (3in) and three 4cm (1½in) canes for the tomato plants. Set all aside to dry.

3 Trim the crust from the cake and slice the top flat. Cut the cake into four equally sized squares and stack one on top of the other. Trim a sloping roof cutting down to the top of the second layer. Sandwich all layers together with buttercream and then spread a thin layer over the surface of the cake as a crumb coat to seal the cake and help the sugarpaste stick. Spread buttercream on the underside of the cake and then position off centre on the cake board.

4 Roll out 200g (7oz) of pale brown sugarpaste and cut a piece to fit the side of the cake, using a ruler to measure correctly. Make the measurement slightly less on the

Mark wood grain with a knife

width due to the indentations stretching the paste. Indent the surface by pressing even lines over the surface using a ruler, taking care not to press too deeply causing the paste to cut. Press the surface with a cake smoother to remove dimples. Set aside for a few moments to firm up before positioning on the cake. Scratch wood grain lines over the surface (**see above**).

5 Cover the opposite side, then the front and back in the same way, securing the joins closed with a little edible glue. Cut out the door on the side four slats width cutting the top slanted following the roof shape. If the door is undamaged after removal, re-use for the door later but if it is, then use as a template to cut another and then set aside to dry.

6 Cut out four squares for the window on the front of the cake and also trim a broken slat at the base of the cake. Roll out the remaining pale brown and cut a piece to cover the top of the cake for the roof, cutting slightly larger than the measurement to create an overlap. Mark slats as before. Cut a hole in the roof using a knife and mark wood grain over the surface of the cake. Cut a ragged edge along the front of the roof to make some planks look old and broken.

7 Thinly roll out black modelling paste and cut pieces to fill the door and windows using the square cutter and cut small pieces to cover the broken areas at the base and on the roof. Score the surface of one window to mark the crack using a knife and then rub the surface of all windows with a little edible silver powder colour to give a glass effect. Using pale brown trimmings cut planks, sticking in place with a small indent at each corner for nail holes using a cocktail stick. Make two planks for the door, sticking in place with a small black handle. Leave the door to dry flat.

8 Roll out the pale grey sugarpaste and cut all the square stepping stones, indenting the surface of each slightly by pinching along the edges. With trimmings, shape flattened circular stepping stones and use to separate the planting sections.

9 To make the water butt, roll 30g (1oz) of green into an oval shape and press down to flatten the top and bottom. Shape 10g (¼oz) into a flattened circle for the lid and mark lines from the centre using the paintbrush handle. Stick a tiny loop of green onto the centre for the handle. Push a hole into the front ready for the tap and then roll a tiny sausage of black modelling paste and stick into the hole, curving it downwards.

10 To make the watering can, roll 10g (¼oz) of green modelling paste into a ball and pinch out a spout at one end, rolling gently between your thumb and index finger. Squeeze to narrow the sides and then push into the top using a bone or ball tool to indent the opening. Roll a small sausage for the handle and press a pea-sized ball flat for the spout, indenting holes using the tip of a cocktail stick. Fill the opening with a little clear piping gel for a water effect and then spread some gel at the base of the water butt.

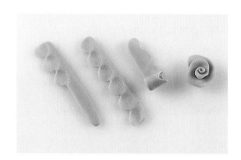

Lettuce stages step-by-step

11 To make the lettuce, first split the pale green into four equal pieces. Roll one piece into a long sausage and roll slightly flat using a rolling pin. Press your finger over the top edge pulling out gently to scallop. Moisten along the bottom and roll up tightly, smoothing open the top **(see above)**. For the runner bean leaves, roll pea-sized amounts of green into tear-drops and roll flat. Press into a leaf veiner to indent and set aside to dry.

12 Cut a small 'v' into the tip of a piping bag. Using the green royal icing pipe little bunches of leaves

in rows by squeezing out the royal icing gently and pulling upwards. Push the tomato canes into the cake board covering and pipe leaves around each one. Push the runner bean canes into the board covering. Cut a small hole in another piping bag and pipe the vines curling around, sticking the dried leaves made earlier in place.

13 To make the scarecrow, first model the slipper and boot. To make the slipper, roll a large pea-sized amount of pale brown modelling paste into a sausage for the sole and roll in the centre rounding off one end slightly larger. Press down to flatten and then press another pea-sized ball on top for the toe area. To make the boot, from 5g (¼oz) of black modelling paste, set aside a pea-sized amount for the glove later and then roll the remainder into an oval shape, pinching up one end for the top of the boot. Push in the end of a paintbrush to open and then cut the front, pinching the flaps out. Mark a line across the top using a knife and around the sole, pushing in with the tip to make the split at the front.

14 For the coat, roll out 25g (just over ¾oz) of the dark cream modelling paste and cut a strip 5 x 10cm (2 x 4in). Wrap around the scarecrow pole turning out the top two corners for lapels **(see above right)**. For the splits in the coat, scratch lines using a knife. Thinly roll out and cut a square for the pocket and stick in place with one side unattached.

Wrap scarecrow coat around pole

15 Set aside a minute amount of dark cream modelling paste for the scarecrow's button nose and then split the remainder in half. Roll into the sausage shaped sleeves, indenting around the end of each for the cuff using a knife. Make a small hole in the end of each sleeve using the end of a paintbrush so the gloves will be held secure. Stick in position with arms outstretched with the jacket and pole placed down flat to dry.

16 Thinly roll out the red modelling paste and cut a 10cm (4in) long strip for the scarf. Make small cuts each end to frill and then wrap around the scarecrow pole at the top of his jacket securing with a little edible glue. Roll the red trimmings into tiny ball shapes for the tomatoes and stick in position. For the gloves, roll a large pea-sized amount of black into a teardrop shape and press slightly flat. Make a cut for the thumb and then three shorter cuts across the top to separate fingers, smoothing along each to remove the cut edge. Pinch at the wrist and then stick into the end of the sleeve. Set aside a tiny amount of blue/grey for the button eye and then make the mitten as the glove, without cutting fingers.

17 To make the scarecrow's head roll the palest brown into a ball and pinch around the bottom to create a ragged edge for the neck. Push in the end of a paintbrush to make a hole ready for the pole later. Press the face down onto the piece of voile to indent a criss-cross pattern or mark gently with a knife. Roll the remaining dark cream into a ball, press flat and indent two holes making the button nose. Repeat for the eyes using black and blue. Roll a tiny very thin sausage of black for his smile. For the hat, roll half of the remaining brown into a ball and press flat for the hat rim, pinching an uneven edge. Stick in place on top of the scarecrow's head with the remaining brown pressed on top. Thinly roll out and cut tiny strips of yellow for hair **(see right)**. Push the head down onto the top of the pole using a little edible glue to secure and then stick the scarecrow in position with the bottom of his pole pushed into the mound on the cake board. If necessary, use pieces of foam to support the arms whilst drying.

18 Brush a little chestnut brown powder colour over the cake board using the no.6 paintbrush. Stick the door in position slightly ajar.

Scarecrow's head step-by-step

Side view

Templates

All templates are 100% actual size.

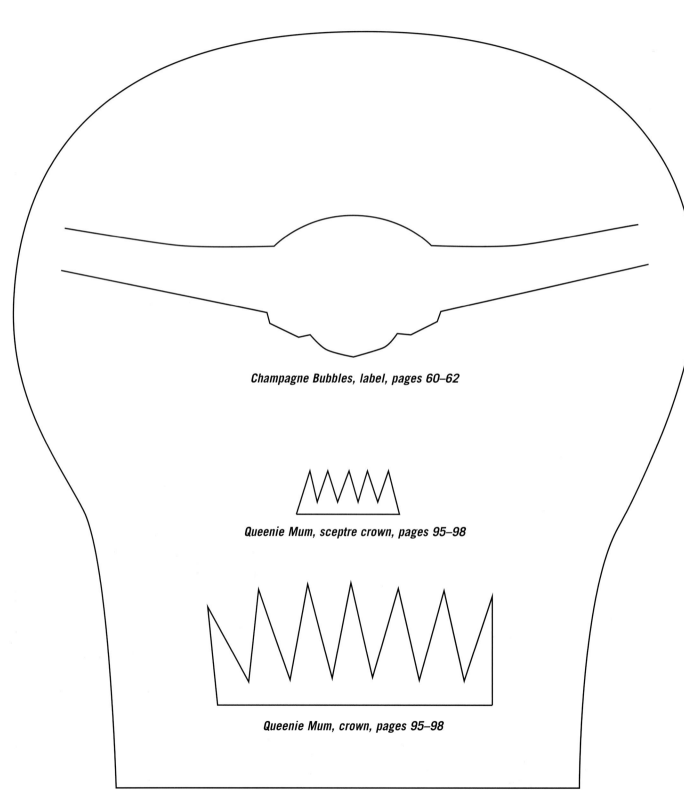

Champagne Bubbles, label, pages 60–62

Queenie Mum, sceptre crown, pages 95–98

Queenie Mum, crown, pages 95–98

Queenie Mum, throne back, pages 95–98

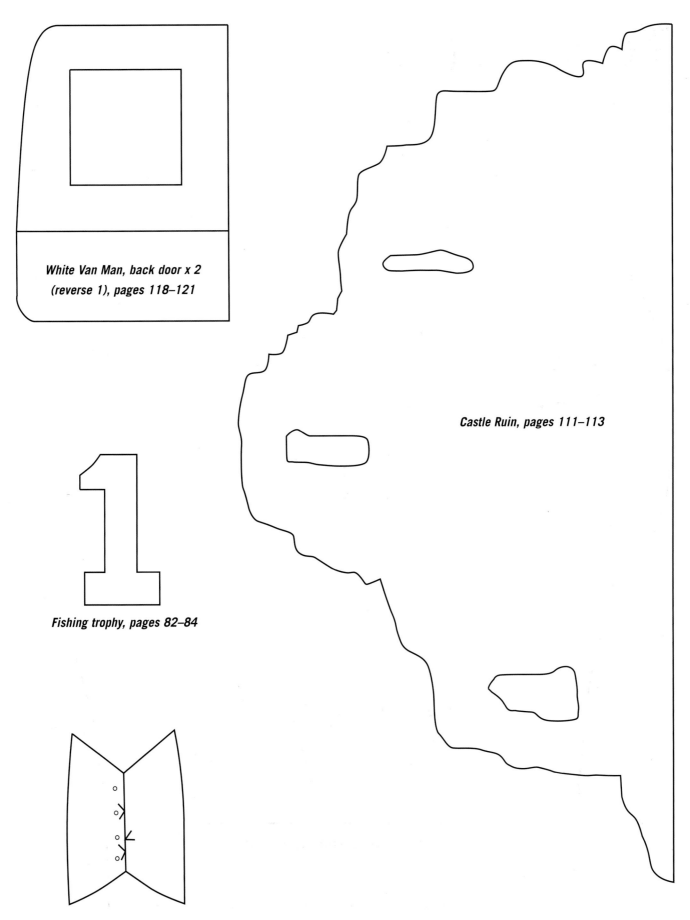

White Van Man, back door x 2
(reverse 1), pages 118–121

Castle Ruin, pages 111–113

Fishing trophy, pages 82–84

Pot of Gold, waistcoat, pages 24–27

Index